GRAPHIC SIMPLICITY

シンプルグラフィックス

GRAPHIC SIMPLICITY
シンプルグラフィックス

PIE BOOKS
2-32-4, Minami-Otsuka, Toshima-ku, Tokyo 170-0005 Japan
Phone: +81-3-5395-4811   Fax: +81-3-5395-4812

e-mail:
editor@piebooks.com
sales@piebooks.com
http://www.piebooks.com

ISBN978-4-89444-623-6 C3070
Printed in Japan

CONTENTS

はじめに

今回、「シンプルグラフィックス」というタイトルを聞いたときに、本全体に表情が出るのかな？と思ったけれど、クール、ナチュラル、スウィート、カラフル、モダンという切り口を設けることによって、ある種の点が見えてきて面白いと感じましたね。デザイン書で「シンプル」というと、大概はポスターとか、パッケージとかで分類しがちですが、普段、切らないような側面から見たらどうなるか。僕たちもシンプルをテーマにものを作るときに、もう一つ軸を決めて考える方法もありだなと思いました。

以前、ファッションデザイナーの森英恵さんが「シンプルは一番難しい」と言っていたんですが、僕もまったく同感です。シンプルは本当にやろうとすると、体力とお金がすごくかかる。これはデザイナーは感じていることだと思いますが、クライアントや消費者の多くは逆だと思ってますよね。一番簡素でコストも安くて済むと。でも、本当にシンプルで手に取って感動するものは、例えば白だけど今まで見たことのないような白さだとか、たった一本の線だけど実はベタじゃないとか、必然なテクニックが存在します。テクニックは必然に基づいていないと、技が浮き上がってシンプルにはならないんです。プロセスが見えると技の見本帳になってしまう。もちろん、頑張らないとダメですが、そこが見えると、シンプルはその瞬間に終わってしまうんです。

今はコンピュータで正確に水平、垂直な線が描けますが、そこに緊張感は感じられません。ディティールが欠けてしまっているんですね。よく「ディティールに神が宿る」みたいなことを言いますが、ディティールが完璧じゃないとシンプルは簡単に崩れさってチープになってしまうと思います。
仕事でよくウェブサイトを使っていますが、広告ではどうしても伝えきれない部分を、ウェブに誘導して伝えればいいわけですから、テレビCMや新聞広告では商品に興味を抱く入口さえ作っておけばいい。となると、広告はどんどんシンプルになっていきます。そうなったときに最後の勝負になるのは、やっぱりディティール。本当は実物を見たり、触れたりする機会があると、よりわかりやすいでしょうね。グラフィックの美しさはもちろんですが、ディティールとか奥行き感とか目に見えないプロセスが集約されたものが、本当に完成されたシンプルだと思います。

プロフィール
内藤 久幹（ないとう ひさもと）
「トーキョウ・グレート・ヴィジュアル」代表
多くのブランドコミュニケーションデザインを手掛けるとともに、「五大陸」「組曲」「満足」「たそがれ清兵衛」「関西リハビリテーション病院」等、数々のブランドアイデンティティを発表。アートを積極的に取り込んだクリエーションデザインは、独自の世界を創り多くの人々に愛され、ヒットブランドとなる。近年、自然・文化を基本としたホスピタリティデザインを提唱。新たなクリエーションとして注目を集めている。

FOREWORD

When I heard the title "Simple Graphics", I wondered if a sense of character would emerge from the book as a whole, but instead thought it would be interesting to reveal certain points or features through the division of entries into the categories of cool, natural, sweet, colorful, and modern. By and large, "simple" design books tend to be categorized by item, such as posters and packaging, but how would it look if we approached it from a less typical angle? It struck me that for us too, there could be an alternative way to produce something on the theme of simplicity: decide on the tone of the material and work from there.

Fashion designer Hanae Mori once commented that "simple" is actually the most difficult to do, a sentiment with which I totally agree. Truly striving to be simple actually requires a huge investment of cash and energy. This is something I suspect all designers feel, whereas most clients and consumers imagine it to be the opposite: that simple is indeed the simplest to do, and the cheapest.
But objects of inspired simplicity inevitably require technique of some sort, whether it be making something all in white a special kind of white never seen before, or drawing a single line that is more than just any old line.
If the technique has no basis in necessity, the skill required to create the item will not come to the fore, and it will not be simple. But if the process is visible, the thing ends up looking like something from a sample book. Yes it's hard, but the moment that hard work can be seen, the simplicity is lost.

These days computers allow us to draw horizontal and vertical lines accurately: the downside being a loss of tension. An absence of detail. They say the devil is in the detail, but the details must be perfect, or simple can easily degrade into simply cheap. We use websites a lot in our job, and because you can direct people to websites when something is impossible to convey in an ad, the TV commercial or newspaper ad now has to provide no more than a gateway to the product that will arouse the viewer's interest. Thus advertising becomes ever more simple. Once this happens, in the end it is the details that make or break the ad. Imagine how much easier it would be to understand if we could actually see and touch the real thing. The beauty of the graphics is vital of course, but to me truly perfect simplicity is the culmination of many factors: detail, depth, and invisible processes.

PROFILE
Hisamoto Naito
Representative Tokyo Great Visual Inc.
As well as working on brand communication design for numerous projects, has created many brand identities including for apparel labels Gotairiku, Kumikyoku and Manzoku, the film Tasogare Seibei (Twilight Samurai) and the Kansai Rehabilitation Hospital. His creative design with its intensely artistic flavor forms a distinctive realm of its own and has become a hit brand in its own right, known and loved by many. In recent years Naito has been an enthusiastic exponent of hospitality design based on natural and cultural elements, and continues to attract new fans with his latest creations.

CREDIT FORMAT
クレジット フォーマット

アイテム名　Items
国　Country
制作年度　Year of production
CL: Client　クライアント
CD: Creative Director　クリエイティブディレクター
AD: Art Director　アートディレクター
D: Designer　デザイナー
P: Photographer　カメラマン
I: Illustator　イラストレーター
CW: Copywriter　コピーライター
DF: Design Firm　デザイン会社
SB: Submittor　作品出品者

＊ 上記以外の制作者呼称は、省略せずに記載しています。
Proffesions except for the above are printed without abbreviation.

＊ 提供者の意向により、クレジットデータの一部を記載していないものがあります。
Some credit data have been omitted at the contributor's requests.

＊各企業名に附随する "株式会社、(株)" 及び "有限会社、(有)" は、省略して記載しています。
The "incorporated" and "limited" portions of Japanese company names have been omitted.

＊広告作品に掲載されている情報は、すでに終了しています。ご了承ください。
The information in the ads shown within are no longer valid.

Simple Cool

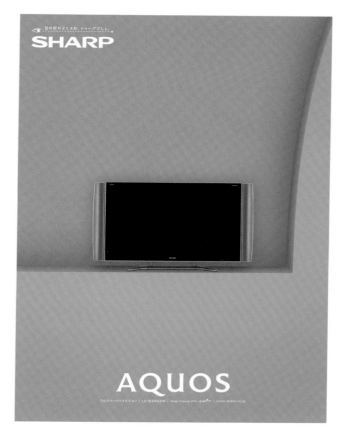

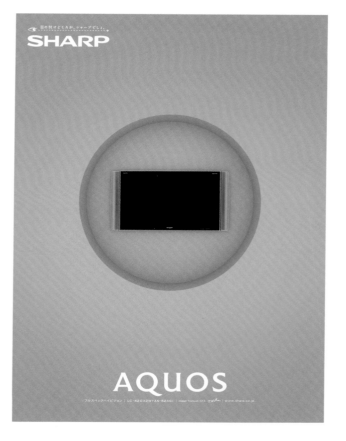

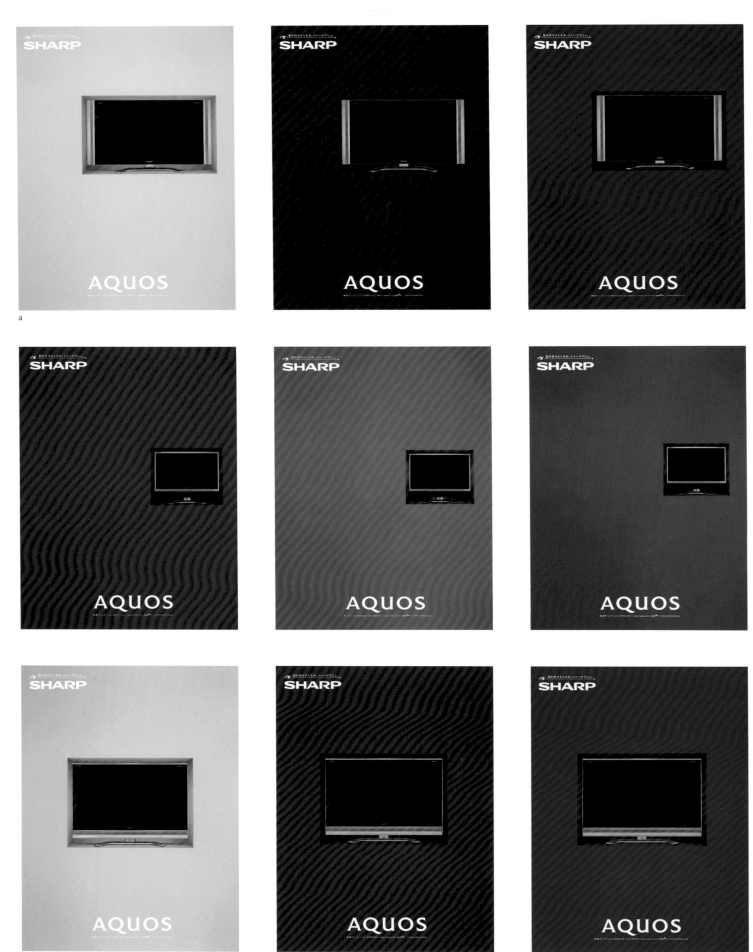

a

Words are a little like icebergs.
Beneath the elegant bits on the
surface is an unseen force holding
everything together. In writing,
this is the thought behind the
words; the strategy that makes
your communication stand out.
So before we put pen to paper, we pause for a while.

**And take a moment to fully understand your aims
and challenges, your company's
brand values and tone of voice,
your audience's attitudes and
behaviour. At these opening stages,
our strategic thought can really
add value. Then, when everything's
in place, we start to write.**

b

We'd all love the luxury of a lazy deadline, some time to
put our feet up. But at ink, we know the clock is always
ticking...

So we work fast:
Teaming up to meet tight deadlines.
Putting two, three or more writers onto large projects.
Using our team to handle sets of marketing literature.
Pooling talents for magazines, ads or branding exercises.
Conducting interviews around the country.
Providing you with your own, dedicated account manager.
And always being available when you need us.

But there's no point in a speedy service if quality slips.
Which is why everything we write is checked by at least
one other member of our team. So the end result is not
just fast, but also flaw-free.

What else do we do?

It's a tough world for words.
For starters there's a lot of them about, jostling for our
attention every day in press, posters, packaging
and online. So we offer a wide range of services
– all linked to our writing expertise – that make words
work that bit harder. Each service is designed to
help build your brand consistency through language
and make sure your marketing's filled with meaning,
not empty promises.

More than you'd expect:

Copy strategy: developing
and implementing a language that reflects your brand.
Training: helping organisations improve writing
skills and express their brand in communications.
Translation: adapting copy for most international
languages using only the best mother-tongue writers.
Editing and proofing: providing a complete editorial
service, from magazine content plans to fully proofing
every item for printing.

a 雑誌広告 Magazine Ad　Japan　2005
　CL: シャープ　SHARP CORPORATION
　CD:安井 健（電通関西支社クリエティブ局）
　　　Ken Yasui (DENTSU INC. Kansai Creativ Direction)
　AD:尾崎 大輔（電通関西支社クリエティブ局）
　　　Daisuke Ozaki (DENTSU INC. Kansai Creativ Direction)
　AD, D, DF: トーキョウ・グレート・ヴィジュアル 大阪
　　　Tokyo Great Visual Inc. Osaka
　P: 青木 健二　Kenji Aoki
　SB: トーキョウ・グレート・ヴィジュアル　Tokyo Great Visual Inc.

b ブローシャー　Brochure　UK　2005
　CL: Ink Copywriters
　AD: Bob Mytton
　D: Tracey Bowes
　CW: Simon Jones / Tom Chcsher
　SB: Mytton Williams

a ポスター Poster
b パッケージ **Package**   Japan 2004
  CL: キリンビバレッジ KIRIN BEVERAGE CORPORATION
  CD, CW: 東 秀紀 Hideki Azuma
  CD, AD: 水野 学 Manabu Mizuno
  D, SB: グッドデザインカンパニー good design company
  CW: 森田 奈津美 Natsumi Morita

b

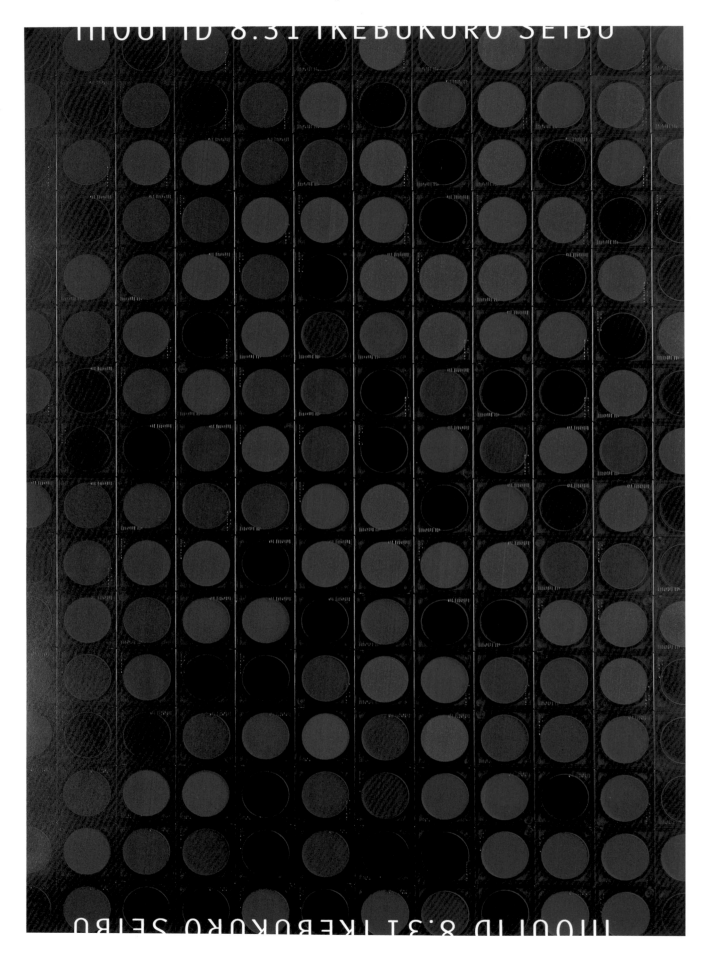

ポスター **Poster** Japan 2006
CL: 資生堂 SHISEIDO CO., LTD.
CD, AD: 渋谷 克彦 Katsuhiko Shibuya
D: 新村 則人 Norito Shinmura
P: 清水 行雄 Yukio Shimizu
DF, SB: 新村デザイン事務所 shinmura design office

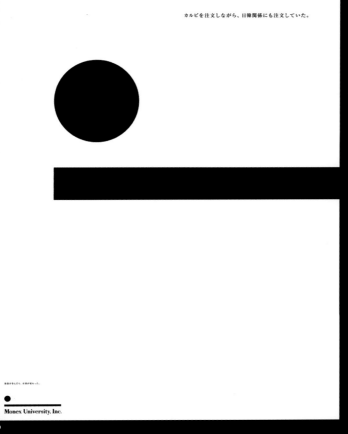

カルビを注文しながら、日韓関係にも注文していた。

Monex University, Inc.

b

次の選曲に迷いながら、次の選挙にも迷っていた。

Monex
University,
Inc.

代表取締役社長
内藤 忍

株式会社 マネックス・ユニバーシティ
〒100-6219 東京都千代田区丸の内1-11-1
パシフィックセンチュリープレイス丸の内19階
Tel 03-6212-3890[代表] Tel 03-6212-3811[直通]
Fax 03-6212-2227
E-mail: naito@monex.co.jp/
http://www.monexuniv.co.jp/

Tomoko Hirosawa
Deputy President

Monex University, Inc.
Pacific Century Place Marunouchi, 19F
1-11-1, Marunouchi, Chiyoda-ku, Tokyo 100-6219, Japan
Tel +81-3-6212-3890[General] +81-3-6212-3888[Direct]
Fax +81-3-6212-2227
[E-mail: hirosawa@monex.co.jp/
http://www.monexuniv.co.jp/]

c

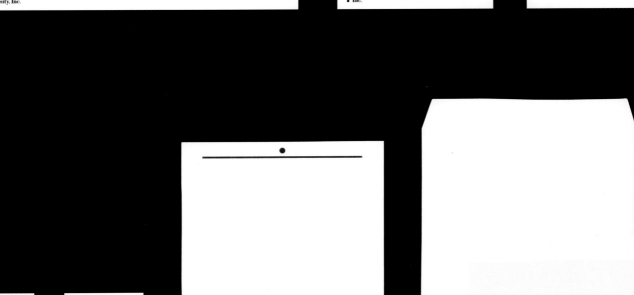

d

Monex University, Inc.

Monex University, Inc.

d

パッケージ Package USA 2004

CL: Parallel Wines Napa Valley
AD: David Schuemann
D: Sara Golzari
P: Tucker and Hossler
DF, SB: CF NAPA

a

b

c

a パッケージ Package   USA 2005

   CL: Klinker Brick
   AD: David Schuemann
   D: Sara Golzari
   P: Tucker and Hossler
   I: Mike Gray
   DF, SB: CF NAPA

b パッケージ Package   USA 2003

   CL: Kesner Wines
   AD: David Schuemann
   D: Liza Butler
   P: Tucker and Hossler
   DF, SB: CF NAPA

c パッケージ Package   USA 2006

   CL: Vinifera Napa Valley
   AD: David Schuemann
   D: Sara Golzari
   P: Tucker and Hossler
   DF, SB: CF NAPA

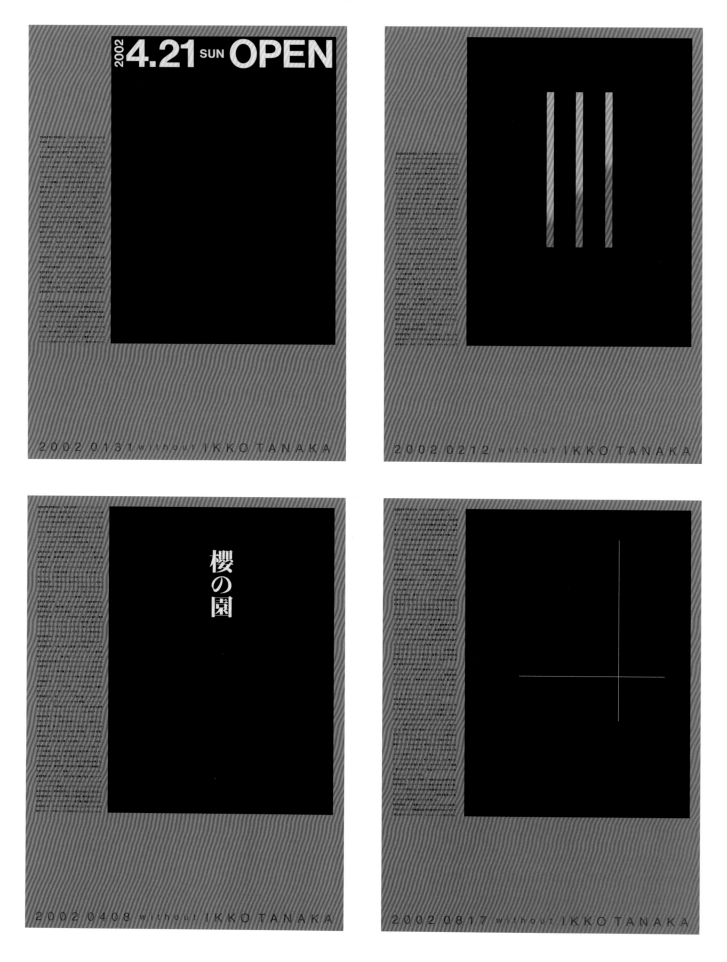

ポスター **Poster** Japan 2002
CL: 特種製紙 TOKUSHU PAPER MFG. Co., Ltd.
CD, AD, D, CW: 木下 勝弘 Katsuhiro Kinoshita
DF, SB: デザイン倶楽部 DESIGN CLUB Inc.

新聞広告　Newspaper Ad　Japan　2003
CL: 三井物産　Mitsui & Co., Ltd.
CD, AD: 川口 清勝　Seijo Kawaguchi
D: 不破 稔　Minoru Fuwa
P: 藤井 保　Tamotsu Fujii
CW: 秋山 晶　Shou Akiyama
DF: BRIDGE
Agency Producer: 佐藤 瑠奈子　Runako Sato / Creative Agency, SB: TUGBOAT

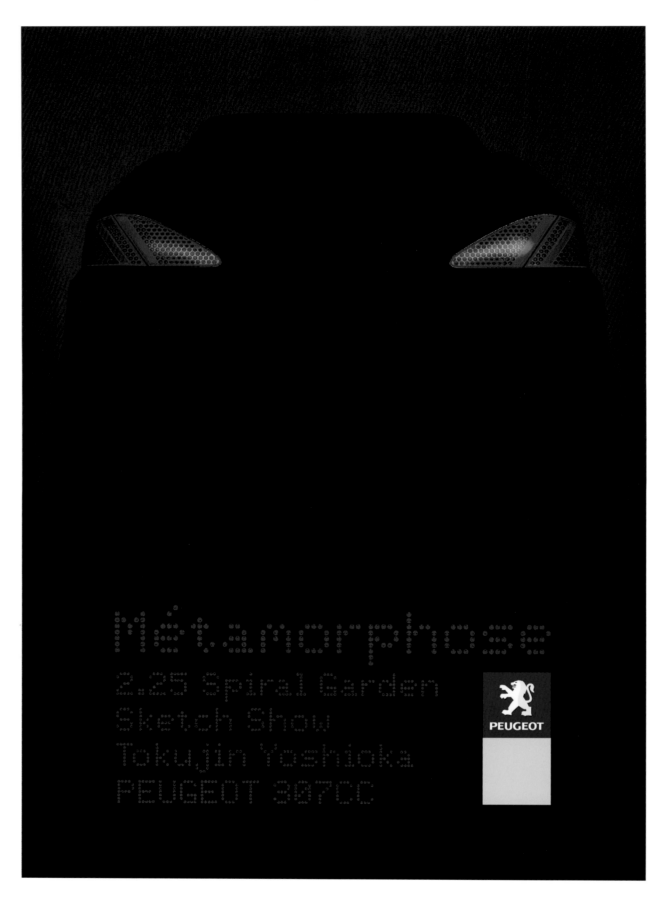

Métamorphose
2.25 Spiral Garden
Sketch Show
Tokujin Yoshioka
PEUGEOT 307CC

ポスター **Poster** Japan 2004
CL: プジョージャポン PEUGEOT Japon Co., Ltd.
CD, AD, D, DF, SB: トーキョウ・グレート・ヴィジュアル Tokyo Great Visual Inc.

a

b

a 雑誌広告 Magazine Ad Japan 2006

CL: Issey Miyake
AD: Florence Bellisson
P: Marcus Tnlinson
Agency: BETC Luxe
SB: BETC Euro RSCG

b 雑誌広告 Magazine Ad Germany 2004～2006

CL: VDZ
AD: Marco Beyer / Sandra Neufeld
CW: Christian Klippel
Agency, SB: McCann Erickson, Hamburg

新聞広告 Newspaper Ad Japan 2004
CL: カッシーナ・イクスシー CASSINA IXC. Ltd.
CD, AD: 日高 英輝 Eiki Hidaka
D: 白須 慎之 Noriyuki Shirasu
　 竹林 一茂 Kazushige Takebayashi
P: MHASUI
CW: 加藤 麻司 Asaji Kato
Retoucher: 桜井 素直 Sunao Sakurai
Agency: アサツーディ・ケイ ASATSU-DK Inc.
DF, SB: グリッツデザイン gritzdesign Inc.

パッケージ **Package**　Japan 2005
CL, SB: 資生堂 SHISEIDO CO., LTD.
AD: 信藤 洋二 Yoji Nobuto
D: 池場 千世 Chiyo Ikeba
CW: 薄 希英 Marehide Susuki

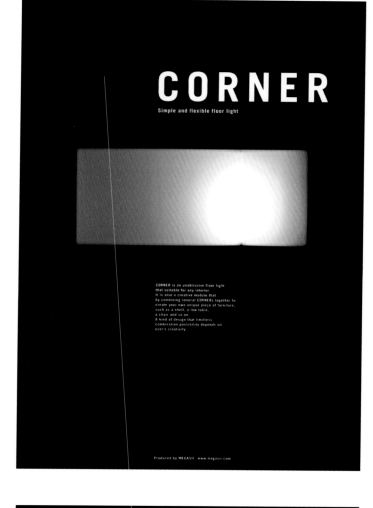

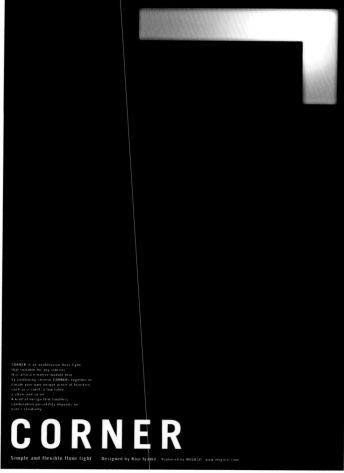

ポスター　Poster　Hong Kong　2005
CL: メガシー　Megasii Limited
AD, D, CW: 居山 浩二　Koji Iyama
CW: 赤土 佳子　Yoshiko Akado / Angeline Wong
DF, SB: イヤマデザイン　iyamadesign

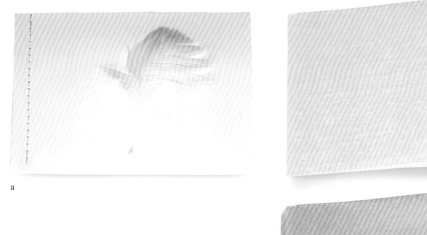

a 招待状 Invitation Italy 2003
CL: FASHION BOX
AD: Joseph Rossi
D, Agency: GraphicFirstAid
Agency, SB: joseph rossi

ジャケットは特殊な素材を使用し、形状を自由に変形させることができる
The book jacket is made of a special material that allows it to take on various forms.

b 書籍 Book Italy 2006
CL, SB: Jekyll & Hyde
AD: Marco Molteni / Margherita Monguzzi
Agency, DF: jekyll & hyde

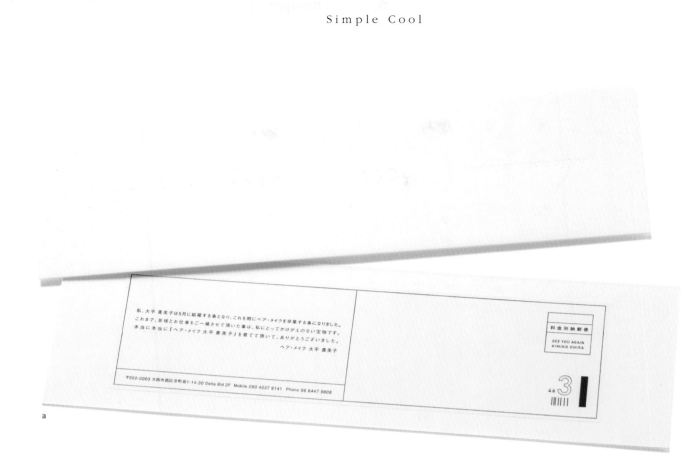

私、大平 貴美子は5月に結婚する事となり、これを期にヘア・メイクを卒業する事になりました。
これまで、皆様とお仕事をご一緒させて頂いた事は、私にとってかけがえのない宝物です。
本当に本当に『ヘア・メイク 大平 貴美子』を育てて頂いて、ありがとうございました。

ヘア・メイク 大平 貴美子

〒550-0003 大阪市西区京町堀1-14-30 Delta Bld 2F Mobile 090 4037 9141 Phone 06 6447 9808

料金別納郵便

SEE YOU AGAIN
KIMIKO OHIRA

46 3

a

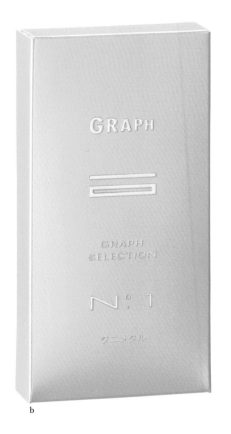

b

c

d

a ダイレクトメール DM Japan 2007

CL: 大平 貴美子 Kimiko Ohira
AD, D: 荻田 純 Jun Ogita
SB: サファリ Safari Inc.

b パッケージ Package Japan 2005

CL, AD, D, SB: グラフ GRAPH Co., Ltd.
AD, D: 北川 一成 Issay Kitagawa

c ペーパーバック Paper Bag
d パッケージ Package Japan 2004

CL: アークレイ ARKRAY, Inc.
AD, D, SB: グラフ GRAPH Co., Ltd.
AD, D: 北川 一成 Issay Kitagawa
AD, D: 松本 悟史 Satoshi Matsumoto

a

a パッケージ **Package**   Japan   2003 ~ 2004

CL, SB: 資生堂 SHISEIDO CO., LTD.
AD: 工藤 青石 Aoshi Kudo
D: 信藤 洋二 Yoji Nobuto

b

b パッケージ **Package** Japan 2006

CL, SB: リサージ LISSAGE Ltd.
CD: 佐藤 可士和 Kashiwa Sato
P: 瀧本 幹也 Mikiya Takimoto

パッケージ **Package** Japan 2005
CL, Agency: サヴィー THAVI Co., Ltd.
CD, AD: 春高 壽人 Hisato Harutaka
D: 門司 大典 Daisuke Monji
DF, SB: 春高デザイン HARUTAKA DESIGN

a

b

a パンフレット　Pamphlet
b パッケージ　Package　Italy 2004

CL: Trattoria Mercato
AD: Michele Salmi
D: Isabella Garlati
P: Marino Ramazzotti
CW: Guido Garlati
Agency: Oikos Associati Visual Communication
SB: Oikos Associati sas

a

b

c

d

a, b パッケージ **Package**　Japan　2007 (a), 2006 (b)
　CL, SB: ブルーベル・ボーテ　Bluebell Beaute K.K
　Total Design Director: 松島 正樹　Masaki Matsushima

c, b パッケージ **Package**　Japan　2004 (c), 2006 (d)
　CL: マンダム　MANDOM CORP
　AD: 重田 元恵　Motoe Shigeta
　D, SB: エイブルデザイン企画　ABLE DESIGN PLANNING Co., Ltd.

パッケージ **Package** Japan 2004

CL, SB: 資生堂 SHISEIDO CO., LTD.
AD: 信藤 洋二 Yoji Nobuto
D: 永田 香 Kaori Nagata

a パッケージ **Package**　Australia　2006

 CL: Yalumba
 AD, D: Annette Harcus
 P: Brenda Read
 Calligraphy: Phoebe Besley / Meg McDonald
 CW: Robert Hill Smith
 DF, SB: Harcus Design

b パッケージ **Package**　Australia　2006

 CL: Tyrrell Wines
 AD: Andrew Hoyne
 D: Laine Warwick
 P: Marcus Struzina
 Agency, DF, SB: Hoyne Design
 Finished Art: Paul Bonacci

a パッケージ **Package**　Australia　2006

CL: Fosters Group
AD: Rainer Bulach
D: Felicity Davison
P: Marcus Struzina
Agency, DF, SB: Hoyne Design
Finished Art: Jim O'neil

b パッケージ **Package**　Canada　2002

CL: LCBO
CD, D: Vanessa Eckstein
DF, SB: Bløk Design

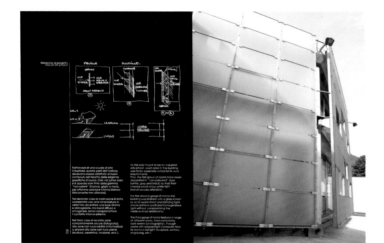

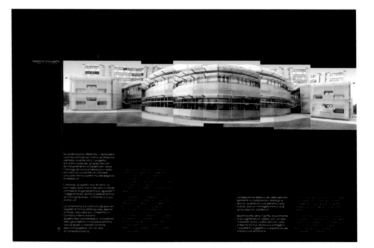

a モノグラフィー **Monography** Italy 2004

CL: OmniDecor
AD, D: Isabella Garlati
AD: Michele Salmi
P: Davide Cerati
Agency: Oikos Associati Visual Communication
SB: Oikos Associati sas

b パンフレット **Pamphlet** Japan 2003

CL: 成安造形大学 SEIAN University of Art and design
CD: 岡田 修二 Shuji Okada
AD, D, SB: 高橋 善丸 Yoshimaru Takahashi
D: 岩本 博 Hiroshi Iwamoto
P: 奥脇 孝一 Koichi Okuwaki
DF: 広告丸 KOKOKUMARU. Co., Ltd.

c カタログ **Catalogue** Japan 2006

CL: イトーキ ITOKI CORPORATION
CD: 菱川 勢一 Sei Hishikawa
D: 三浦 健太 Kenta Miura
P: 斎藤 裕貴 (スタジオワンキャラット) / Yuki Saito (Studio One Carat Inc.)
CW: 松永 芳典 Yoshinori Matsunaga
Producer: 近藤 里恵子 Rieko Kondo
DF, SB: スタンダード・シリーズ STANDARD SERIES

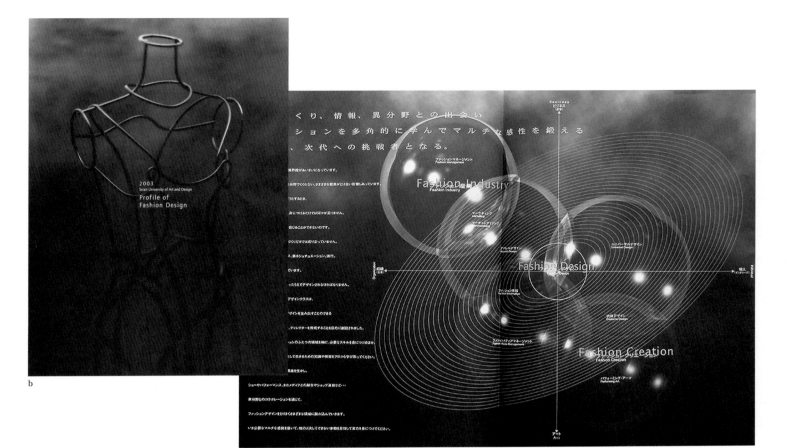

b

c

S/S06 show

Masako Endo:assistant/Kana Fujii:fitting model/Rie Hanafusa:assistant/Jun Hayashida:salesclerk/HYPE:casting/Yoshihiro Hatamoto:modelist
Tomoko Iijima:assistant/Tetsuya Inoue:assistant/Kenta Ishihara:assistant/Ohko Ishida:Hat designer/Akemi Kagaya:accountant
Masaki Kaneda:japan sales/Hironori Kawauchi:press/Masahiro Koyama:president/Takafumi Kusagaya:art director
Rie Maeda:salesclerk/Ato Matsumoto:designer/Akiko Miura:japan sales/Shinya Miura:salesclerk/Akihiro Mishouyama:Production
Chihoko Nakanishi:press support/Kenichiro Nishihara:sound creator/Keisuke Nishitani:modelist/Hideki Osugi:modelist/Junko Sakayori:modelist
Makoto Sasagawa:japan sales/Hiroko Sasaki:salesclerk/SAT:shoe maker/Akihiko Sekigawa:salesclerk/John Storey:international sales
Makio Tanioka:show director/Yukiko Utsumi:accountant/Arifumi Wada:japan sales/Takumi Yamamoto:Production/Kiyoshi Yoneno:modelist
Special thanks to:
Tokyo District Conference Of Tanning Industry/SIC,Shindo Senikogyo Co.,Ltd/life

ato press office #706 5-4-35 Minami-Aoyama Minato-ku Tokyo Japan 107-0062 T/81.3 54 68 51 37 F/81.3 54 68 51 36 U/www.ato.jp

b

ato spring/summer 06 collection for women (+men)

tuesday 1 november 05

door open 20:00 show time 20:30

place:Kurenai at the meiji memorial picture gallery

contact:ato press office 03-5468-5137

contact on 1 november Japan Fashion Strategy Forum 03-5645-8210

1-1 kasumigaokacho shinjyuku-ku tokyo

ato autumn/winter 04 collection for women (+men) exhibition

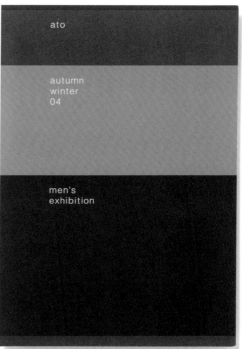

ato

autumn
winter
04

men's
exhibition

c

ダイレクトメール DM   Japan   2005 (a, b), 2004 (c)

CL: アトウ ato
AD, D: 草谷 隆文 Takafumi Kusagaya
D: 金坂 義之 Yoshiyuki Kanesaka
DF, SB: 草谷デザイン Kusagaya Design Inc.

'07 Spring PremierBLACK Fair

M-premierBLACK
www.m-premier.jp

'07 Spring PremierBLACK Fair

2007.3.17 sat.-3.25 sun.

Present

M-premierBLACK

M-premierBLACK

M-PREMIER

'07 Spring Premier Fair

M-PREMIER

'07 Spring Premier Fair

M-PREMIER

2007.3.10 sat.-3.18 sun.

Present

ダイレクトメール DM Japan 2007
CL: エム・アイ・ディー mid Co., Ltd.
D: 門田 聡子 Satoko Kadota
DF, SB: ネイムス names Inc.

パッケージ Package Japan 2007
CL: ゴンチャロフ製菓 Goncharoff Confectionery Co., Ltd.
CD: ゴンチャロフ製菓 企画部 Goncharoff Planning Dept.
AD, D: 永島 学 Manabu Nagashima
D: 高山 マキコ Makiko Takayama
SB: 永島学デザイン室 Manabu Nagashima Design Inc.

a

a アニュアルレポート **Annual Report** USA 2003

    CL: Underwriters Laboratories Inc.
    AD: Ted Stoik
    AD, D: Tim Hartford / David Wozniak
    P: Various
    DF: Dovetail Communications
    DF, SB: Hartford Design
    DF: Woz Design

b CD Japan 2004

    CL: 梯 郁夫 Ikuo Kakehashi
    AD, D: 永井 裕明 Hiroaki Nagai
    D: 岩田 勇紀 Yuki Iwata
    P: 市川 勝弘 Katsuhiro Ichikawa
    Producer: 伊藤 圭一 Keiichi Ito
    DF, SB: エヌ・ジー N.G. Inc.

c カタログ **Catalogue** Singapore 2006

    CL: Singapore Institute of Archtects
    AD: Torrance Goh
    D: Christina Chia / Darrell Lim
    CW: Tania De Rozario
    DF, SB: Octopus Printers

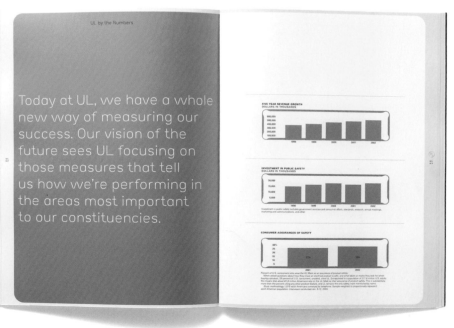

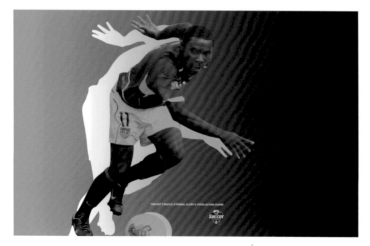

ポスター Poster   USA 2005

CL: Fox Soccer Channel
AD: Bill Thorburn
D: Steve Jockisch, Terese Corredato
CW: Glen Wachowiak, Steve Casey, Jonathan Graham
DF, SB: Carmichael Lynch Thorburn

カタログ **Catalogue**   Italy   2006 (a), 2007 (b)
CL: NEW MIILS
AD: Joseph Rossi
D, Agency: GraphicFirstAid
P: Giuliano Francesconi
Agency, SB: joseph rossi

a カタログ Catalogue Japan 2006
CL: ロートレアモン LAUTREAMONT Co., Ltd.
AD, D: 堀口 秀司 Shuji Horiguchi
D: 門田 聡子 Satoko Kadota / 岡田 藍 Ai Okada
P: 中川 真人 Makoto Nakagawa
SB: ネイムス names Inc.

b 装丁 Book Cover Japan 2004
CL: アウトバーン Autobahn Ltd.
CD: 小泉 雅史 Masafumi Koizumi
AD: 中島 浩 Hiroshi Nakajima
DF, SB: プランク Plank Co., Ltd.

c 装丁 Book Cover Japan 2007
CL: 日本産業デザイン振興会
Japan Industrial Design Promotion Organization
AD, D, SB: 工藤 強勝 Tsuyokatsu Kudo
D: 伊藤 滋章 Shigeaki Ito
Supervision: 森山 明子 Akiko Moriyama
DF: デザイン実験室 Design Laboratory

a

a 招待状 Invitation
b カタログ Catalogue   Japan 2007
CL: シャネル CHANEL K.K.
AD: 美澤 修 Osamu Misawa
D: 竹田 麻衣子 Maiko Takeda
SB: 美澤修デザイン室 osamu misawa designroom Co., Ltd.

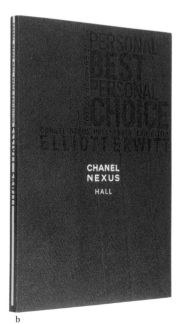

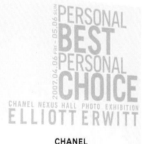

b

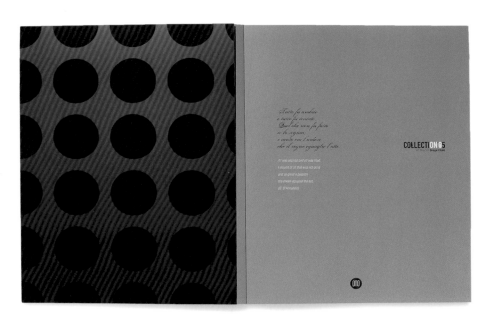

カタログ Catalogue　Italy　2005

CL: Ono Luce
AD: Joseph Rossi
D, Agency: GraphicFirstAid
P: Officina Luce / Giustino Chemello
Agency, SB: joseph rossi

ジャケットは袋状になっていてスタッフの顔が印刷
されたシートが入っている
The jacket forms a sleeve into which sheets printed
with portraits of the staff are inserted.

会社案内　Company Brochure　Italy　2007
CL: Interpool
AD: Joseph Rossi
D, Agency: GraphicFirstAid
Agency, SB: joseph rossi

a

b

a パッケージ **Package**　USA　2005

　CL: Teague
　AD, D: Ben Graham / Steve Watson
　P: Dong Evans
　DF, SB: Turnstyle

b ダイレクトメール　**DM**　Japan　2005

　CL: オリンパス　Olympus Corporation
　AD: 大野 耕平　Kohei Ohno
　D: 中島 裕治　Yuji Nakajima
　CW: 追川 知紀　Tomonori Oikawa
　Agency: 博報堂　HAKUHODO Inc.
　DF, SB: 博報堂プロダクツ　HAKUHODO PRODUCTS

c パッケージ **Package** Japan 2005
CL: アスクル ASKUL Corporation
AD, CW: 田代 嘉宏 Yoshihiro Tashiro
D: 中山 祐香 Yuka Nakayama
DF, SB: ゴースト GOEST, Inc.

d 展覧会図録 **Exhibition Record** Japan 2003
CL: サントリーミュージアム［天保山］ SUNTORY MUSEUM, Osaka
AD, D: シマダ タモツ Tamotsu Shimada
P: 奥脇 孝一 Koichi Okuwaki
SB: シマダデザイン Shimada Design Inc.

c

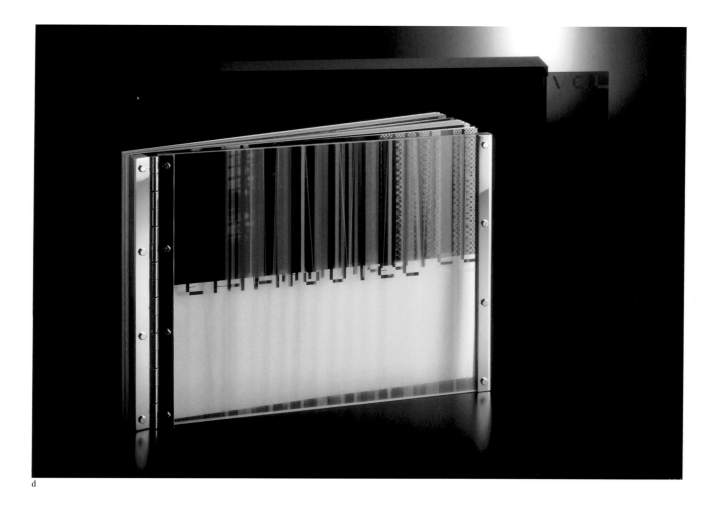

d

8/19 Renewal Open

We would like to express our sincere appreciation for your continued support.
It is a pleasure to announce the renewal open of our shop. We hope you will
come and enjoy this celebration.
http://www.m-premier.jp/

m, i, d, shop

9/20 → 25 PREMIER FAIR

We would like to express our sincere appreciation for your continued support.
It is a pleasure to announce "Premier Fair".
We hope you will come and enjoy this celebration.
... and "MiO 10th Anniversary"

M-PREMIER

9/23 → 27 PREMIER FAIR

We would like to express our sincere appreciation for your continued support.
It is a pleasure to announce "Premier Fair".
We hope you will come and enjoy this celebration.
http://www.m-premier.jp/

M-PREMIER

the **1**st
Anniversary FAIR of Reopening
2005.02.25.FRI. >>>
2005.03.06.SUN.

伊勢丹新宿店本館2階
=ヤングスポーツウェア / M-プルミエが、
リフレッシュオープン1周年を迎えます。

リフレッシュオープン1周年を記念して、
2005年2月25日(金)〜3月6日(日)の間、
お買いあげ31,500円以上の
お客さまに先着400名さまにオリジナルTシャツを
ご用意いたしております。
皆さまのご来店を心よりお待ちしております。
尚、当日はこのDMをご持参ください。

ダイレクトメール DM Japan 2005
CL: エム・アイ・ディー mid Co., Ltd.
D: 門田 聡子 Satoko Kadota
DF, SB: ネイムス names Inc.

a ビジネスカード Business Card USA 2005
　CL: Cypress
　DF: Gouthier Design : A Brand Collective
　SB: Gouthier Design

b 名刺 Business Card UK 2003
　CL: DSFX
　AD, D: Paul West
　D: Chris Hilton
　DF, SB: Form

c 名刺 Business Card UK 2002
　CL, DF, SB: Form
　AD, D: Paul West / Paula Benson
　D: Nick Hard

d ステーショナリー Stationery Canada 2004
　CL: Shan
　AD, D: Maxime Levesque
　DF, SB: Levesque Design

30 Years of Service Episcopal Group Homes, Inc.

egh**30**

Episcopal Group Homes, Inc. provides quality residential services to persons with developmental disabilities. EGH programs and staff members create a supportive and challenging environment so that clients can develop skills essential to functioning as members of a community.

Independence. Episcopal Group Homes recognizes that an individual's level of independence can have a direct effect on his or her self-esteem, and that self-esteem can be a determining factor in motivation and learning. Independence in this sense is not only defined by a physical living environment, but also own life decisions as well as the number and quality of that person's relationships with others.

Philosophy. The philosophy of EGH strongly encourages skill development, relationship building and self-determination, as opposed to simply providing a protective environment. Training in self-help and social skills, along with opportunities to experience the natural consequences of decisions and behavior, promote growth toward maximum self-sufficiency.

1 Mission

a

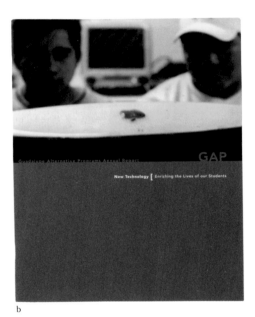

Guadalupe Alternative Programs Annual Report   GAP

New Technology | Enriching the Lives of our Students

b

Mission

[Mission

Guadalupe Alternative Programs fosters learning, personal growth and skill development in those individuals who are not well served by mainstream educational institutions.

[**History** Guadalupe Alternative Programs was founded in 1967 as a school for dropouts when Sister M. Giovanni Gourhan and the School Sisters of Notre Dame, the Catholic Order of Sisters to which she belonged, purchased a house near Our Lady of Guadalupe Church on St. Paul's West Side. In 1970, a nine-room building was added to the house. More than 50 young persons attended the alternative school. In 1989, construction of a four-story building was completed and the Guadalupe Alternative Programs' school enrollment doubled. Adult literacy classes in the new building and other programs were expanded. In 1995, more space was added, including a gymnasium, classroom space to accommodate a junior high school program, computer lab, industrial arts and day care. Enrollment increased to 160.

[**Vision and Uniqueness** GAP provides a compassionate, respectful and nurturing educational environment that helps young people over the barriers of poverty, racism and self-destructive behavior — obstacles that prevent them from living productive and successful lives. GAP has a 30-year history of serving young people and adults on St. Paul's West Side. Its teachers, counselors and administrators are uniquely suited and equipped to provide educational and social opportunities to its community. GAP has demonstrated consistently that its programming, based on relationship and trust, is successful over time. Small class size and attention to cultural uniqueness are primary considerations as teachers nurture the educational and leadership potential of their students.

[**Diversity** GAP welcomes persons of all races, creeds, ages, genders, sexual orientations and national origins and is prepared to serve persons with disabilities. The ethnic composition of the West Side neighborhoods served by the Guadalupe Alternative Programs is predominately Chicano/Latino, but includes people of many races and creeds. GAP programming is adaptable and serves its changing constituency. Students attending the alternative school, for instance, come from many St. Paul neighborhoods, including the Lower East Side, Selby/Dale and Frogtown. GAP celebrates the positive and distinctive characteristics of its diverse community and participates in various cultural ceremonies and traditions. GAP also acknowledges that some characteristics of that community summon our concern. These constants have been observed in populations served by GAP:

[ ] Approximately 90 percent of the students attending Guadalupe Alternative Programs receive lunch subsidies.
[ ] Families served live in neighborhoods where poverty is deep and chronic.
[ ] Many of the families served live in sub-standard or "transitional" housing.
[ ] All of the individuals and families served come from neighborhoods where crime and violence are everyday realities.

[11]

[Financial

$$$

[Board of Directors

Coulette Columbus-Powers, Chair
Art Guerrero
Paul Jacques
Sr. Rita Jirik
Sheila Johnson, Secretary
Kim Kusnier
Yvonne Lee
Jane Peterson, Treasurer
Rebecca Rojas
Dave Swanson
Karen Thompson, Vice Chair

[Administration

Allen Selinski, Executive Director
Jody Nelson, Associate Director
Margaret Mazzaferro, Director of Administration
Marie Capra, Director of Youth and Family Services

[Income
State Grants $ 1,195,384
Other Gov.t Grants $ 446,172
Foundation Grants $ 23,100
Contributions $ 96,812
United Way $ 205,718
Special Events $ 12,742
Other Income $ 115,834

[Expenses
Salaries, Benefits, Training $ 1,674,818
Buildings and Equipment $ 94,805
Supplies, Printing, Phone $ 127,412
Depreciation $ 91,434
Miscellaneous $ 5,712

a アニュアルレポート **Annual Report** USA 2006
　CL: Episcopal Group Homes, Inc.
　AD, D: William Homan
　CW: Tom Helgeson
　DF, SB: William Homan Design

b アニュアルレポート **Annual Report** USA 2002
　CL: Guadalupe Alternative Programs
　AD, D: William Homan
　CW: Tom Helgeson
　DF, SB: William Homan Design

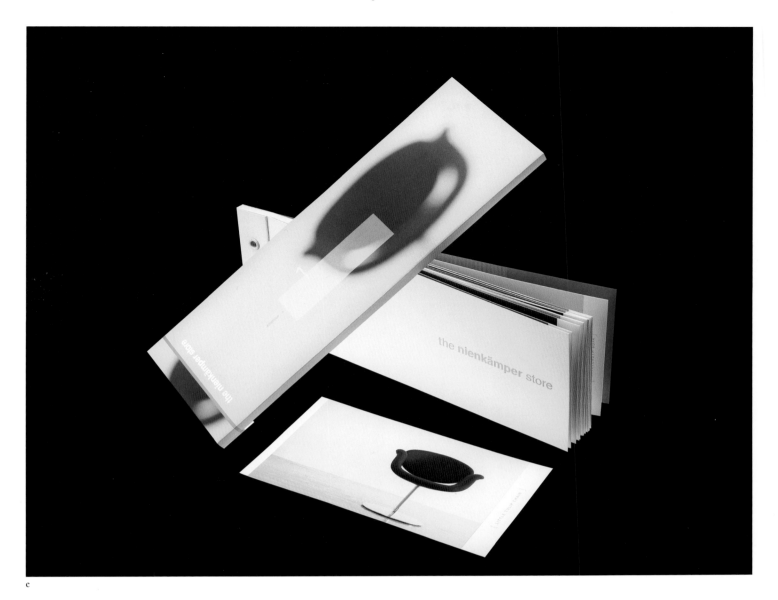

c

d

c カタログ **Catalogue**　Canada 2002

  CL: Nienkamper
  CD, D: Vanessa Eckstein
  D: Frances Chen
  P: Antoine Boote
  DF, SB: Bløk Design

d ダイレクトメール　**DM (CD)**　Japan 2007

  CL: クオミスト　QUOMIST
  D: 中谷 紳介　Shinsuke Nakatani
  DF: ブッチ・プラニング　Butch Planning
  SB: プラザスタイル　PLAZASTYLE

ニューイヤーズ ブックレット
New Years Booklet   Austria   2004

CL, DF, SB: Felder Grafikdesign
AD, D: Peter Felder
CW: Dennis Genpo Merzel

Simple Natural

a

b

FEBRUARY
FEBRUAR
FEVRIER
FEBBRAIO
FEBRERO

a 書籍 Book
b カレンダー Calendar   Japan 2005 (a), 2003 (b)
  CL: 三井物産 Mitsui & Co., Ltd.
  CD, AD: 川口 清勝 Seijo Kawaguchi
  D: 不破 稔 Minoru Fuwa
  P: 藤井 保 Tamotsu Fujii
  CW: 秋山 晶 Shou Akiyama
  Producer: 小川 積明 Noriaki Ogawa (b)
  DF: BRIDGE
  Agency Producer: 佐藤 瑠奈子 Runako Sato / Creative Agency, SB: TUGBOAT
  publish: リトル・モア Little more (a)

Poster Japan 2005
CL: 中島総合文化センター Nakajima Culture Center
AD, D: 溝田 明 Akira Mizota
P: 嵯山 ゆり Yuri Sayama
CW: 清野 かほる Kahoru Seino
SB: デザインエイエム designam Co., Ltd.

ポスター　Poster　Japan　2004
CL: WALL
AD: 副田 高行　Takayuki Soeda
D: 貝塚 智子　Tomoko Kaizuka
P: 泊 昭雄　L.A. Tomari
SB: 副田デザイン制作所　SOEDA DESIGN FACTORY

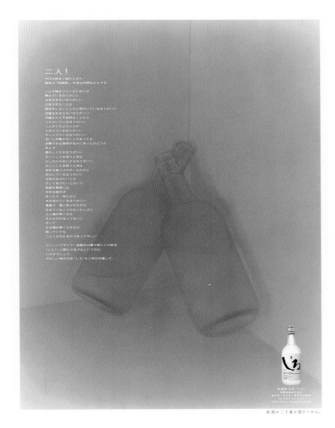

新聞広告 Newspaper Ad   Japan 2005
CL: 高橋酒造 TAKAHASHI SYUZOU
CD, AD: 副田 高行（副田デザイン制作所）/ Takayuki Soeda (SOEDA DESIGN FACTORY)
CD, CW: 松木 圭三（マーキュリー・アンド・マカリスター・オオサカ）Keizo Matsuki (Mercury + McAllister Osaka)
　　　　伏屋 雅美（副田デザイン制作所）Masami Fuseya (SOEDA DESIGN FACTORY)
P: 泊 昭雄 Akio Tomari
Agency, SB: 熊日広告社 Kumanichi Koukokusha Inc.

BRADFORD

TrendScape

a

Juiced-UP

Playful stacks of vibrantly colored soap slabs punctuated, scented with delicious fruit pieces for a naturally fragrant of scash Mango, Blackberry, Passion Fruit, Lime and Peach. As an added benefit these pieces contain vitamins and antioxidants.

The Peach flavored soap was formulated with DayGlow™ Blaze Orange for extra brilliant color. The jellied appearance of the Passion Fruit and Lime flavored soaps was created using proprietary additives in our vegetable translucent base.

20/20

Whimsical, eye-popping soap flowers created using Bradford's state-of-the-art PC-500 glycerin base. Because it is water-white and crystal-clear, PC-500 provides the clearest viewing in the industry. PC-500 is virtually odorless, so you can really respond to all these delicately fragranced flowers. They were manufactured by inserting colorful opaque flower-shaped soaps between two layers of fruit-patterned PC-500.

a ブローシャー　Brochure
b ポスター　Poster　USA 2003

CL: Bradford Soap Works
AD: Tom Laidlaw
D: Arvi Raquel-Santos / Brad Lewthwaite
P: John Van S. / Michael Weymouth
DF, SB: Weymouth Design

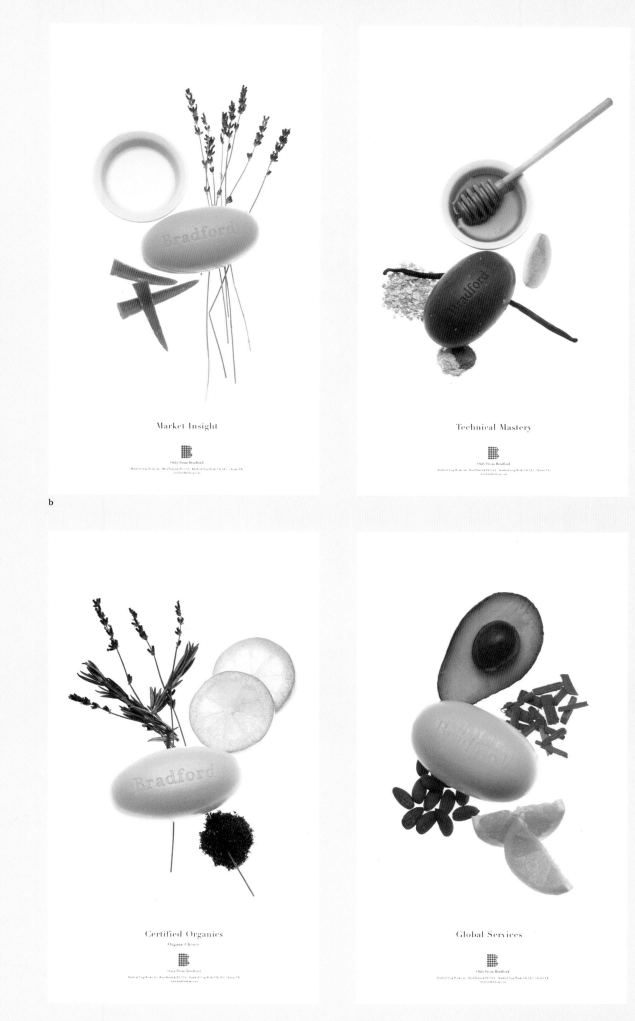

Market Insight

Technical Mastery

Certified Organics

Global Services

b

雑誌広告 Magazine Ad   France   2006

CL: Air France
AD: Eric Holden
P: Jonathan de Villiers
CW: Remi Noel
Agency, SB: BETC Euro RSCG

ポスター Poster

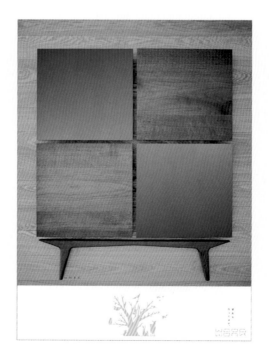

ポスター **Poster** Japan 2007
CL: 下甚商店 SHIMOJIN SHOTEN Co., Ltd.
CD, AD, D, P: 関 宙明 Hiroaki Seki
CW: フジタノリコ NorikoFujita
DF, SB: ミスター・ユニバース Mr. Universe

ジェネラルグラフィック **General Graphic** Japan 2005

CL: Pd Ltd./紙館島勇 Pd Ltd./Kamiyakata Shimayu Ltd.
AD, P: 加藤 建吾 Kengo Kato
D: 山田 靖子 Yasuko Yamada / 竹中 智博 Tomohiro Takenaka / 新井 崇 Takashi Arai / 草野 剛 Tsuyoshi Kusano
P: 宮本 敬文 Keibun Miyamoto
DF, SB: TUGBOAT2

パンフレット **Pamphlet** Japan 2006
CL: 旭化成ホームズ Asahi Kasei Homes Corporation
CD, AD: 松下 計 Kei Matsushita
D: 高田 恵子 Keiko Takada
P: 望月 孝 Takashi Mochizuki
I: 大塚 いちお Ichio Otsuka
CW: 栗原 慶子 Keiko Kurihara
SB: 松下計デザイン室 KEI Matsushita Design Room Inc.

Nature for Urban Life

エコロジーと、ここちよい生活。
どちらも大切だからこそ、
都市の住まいには
"自然"が必要です。

6

「地球にやさしく、人にここちよい住まい」を求めて。

地球はいま、さまざまな環境問題を抱えています。
とりわけ深刻な温暖化の進行をくいとめるため、2005年には「京都議定書」が発効。
世界各国が、CO₂（二酸化炭素）など温室効果ガス排出削減の努力を続けています。
また私たちが暮らす日本の都市も、ヒートアイランド現象をはじめ、
生活環境の悪化という悩みを抱えているのが実情。
こうした問題を背景に、住まいにハイレベルな環境配慮が求められるようになり、
年間暖冷房負荷の低減を目的とした省エネルギー基準の改正・強化が、たびたび行われました。
健康と住環境との関係にもますます関心が高まっており、
「地球にやさしく、人にここちよい住まい」が求められています。

↓

ヘーベルハウスは、その答えを、"自然"のなかにみつけました。

「地球にやさしく、人にここちよい住まい」を実現するために。
ヘーベルハウスは住まいづくりにあたり、3つのことを大切にしています。
基本になるのは、廃棄物削減につながる【建物の長期耐用化】。
構造躯体や設計手法などの研究・開発により、
新築時の住み心地を半世紀以上も保つ「ロングライフ住宅」を実現しています。
そして設計上の配慮・提案による、住まいへの【自然の恵みの活用】です。
自然の恵みを活かすことは、地球環境と人との
サスティナブル（持続可能）な関係を築く鍵となります。
さらに、地球や自然にやさしい【住まい方の工夫】もご提案。
このあと【自然の恵みの活用】【住まい方の工夫】についてお話ししていきます。
お客様の大切な住まいづくりに、ぜひお役立てください。

(建物の
長期耐用化)　(自然の恵みの
活用)　(住まい方の
工夫)

7

ヘーベルハウスには、
都市の一邸一邸に"自然の恵み"を最大限に活かす
さまざまなテクノロジーがあります。

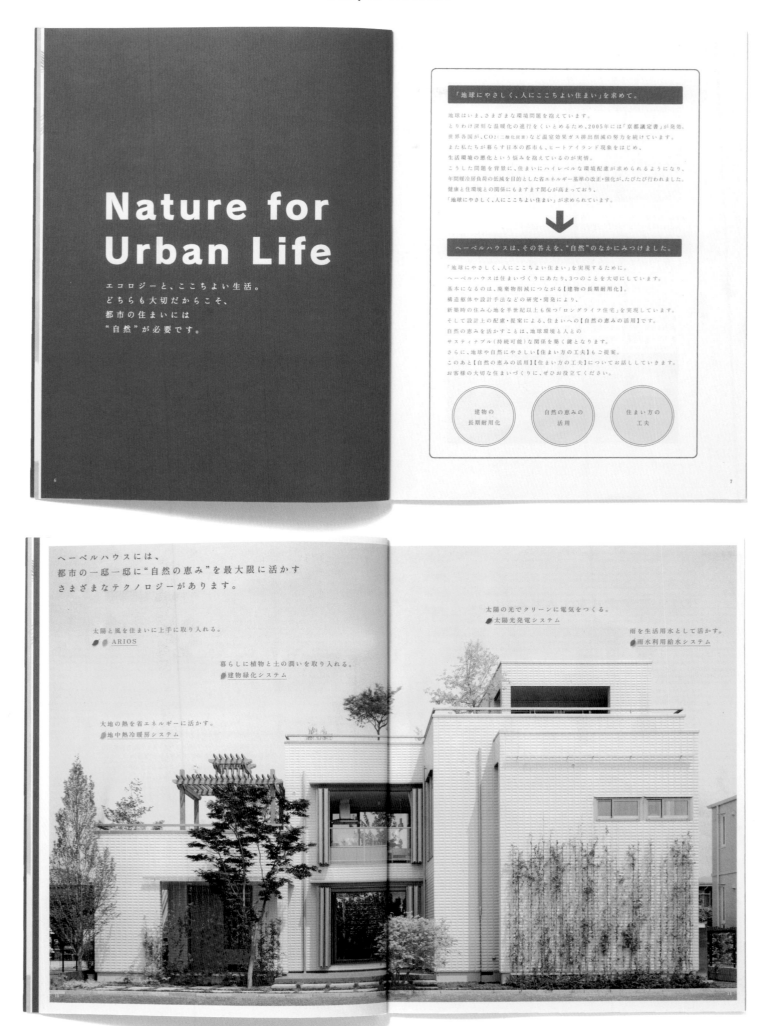

太陽の光でクリーンに電気をつくる。
◢ 太陽光発電システム

太陽と風を住まいに上手に取り入れる。
◢ ARIOS

雨を生活用水として活かす。
◢ 雨水利用給水システム

暮らしに植物と土の潤いを取り入れる。
◢ 建物緑化システム

大地の熱を省エネルギーに活かす。
◢ 地中熱冷暖房システム

ポスター Poster Japan 2006
CL: 名古屋鉄道 Nagoya Railroad Co., Ltd.
CD, CW: 加藤 文敏 Fumitoshi Kato
AD: 長谷川 辰郎 Tatsuro Hasegawa
D: 冨田 修平 Shuhei Tomida
P: tatsuro
Agency, SB: 電通名鉄コミュニケーションズ
　　　　　DENTSU MEITETSU COMMUNICATIONS INC.
DF: たきグラフィックス TAKI GRAPHICS CORPORATION

Happy Birth Time

年に一度、誕生日が来るように、
一日に一度、誕生時間が来ます。
あなたは何時何分に
この世に生まれましたか？
あれは寒い夜中だった…。
夏の熱い昼下がりだった…。
そのときの母のぬくもりを、
父のまなざしを、
想像してみませんか？
さあ、もうすぐあなたが生まれた時間ですよ。
お誕生時間、おめでとう。

ポスター　Poster　Japan　2007
CL: 長野時計店　NAGANO TOKEITEN Co., Ltd.
CD: 平野 大輔　Daisuke Hirano
AD: 梶原 道生　Michio Kajiwara
D: 中島 めぐみ　Megumi Nakashima
P: 前田 真三　Shinzo Maeda
CW: 松田 正志　Masashi Matsuda
Agency: 三広　SANKO
DF, SB: カジグラ　KAJIGRA
DF: 広告研究所　KOUKOKU KENKYUSHO

ポスター　Poster　Japan　2004
CL: フォルクスワーゲングループジャパン　Volkswagen Group Japan
CD: Ken Trevor
AD: 窪田 雅一　Masakazu Kubota
P: 位田 明夫　Akio Inden
I: 宗戸 一眞　Kazuma Muneto
Agency, SB: DDB 東急エージェンシークリエイティブ　DDB Tokyu Agency Creative
DF: ゴーズ　GOES Inc.

ポスター Poster　Germany　2003

CL: WWF Worldwide Fund for Nature
AD: Simon Oppmann / Esra Paola Crugnale
CW: Peter Roemmelt
Agency, SB: Ogilvy Frankfurt

カタログ　Catalogue　Japan　2006
CL, SB: イデア インターナショナル　IDEA International Co., Ltd.
AD: 得能 正人　Masato Tokuno

KENZOKI SKINCARE THAT MAKES YOU FEEL GOOD

豊かな自然の恩恵を受け、多くの栄養成分を含んでいること。
そして、情緒的部分にやさしく働きかける香りを持っていること。
この二つの要素を絶妙なハーモニーであわせ持つ四つの植物を厳選しました。
KENZOKIはそれぞれの植物の個性を壊すことなく、そのまま引き出しています。

どこまでも潔く、茎はあくまで瑞々しく。

KI ENERGIZING — BAMBOO LEAF

その花は艶麗と香り、心躍らせる。

KI EUPHORIC — GINGER FLOWER

やさしく、やわらかく。水面に揺蕩う花のように。

KI RELAXING — WHITE LOTUS

甘美な香りは、艶への誘い。陶然と身を委ねる快さ。

KI SENSUAL — RICE STEAM

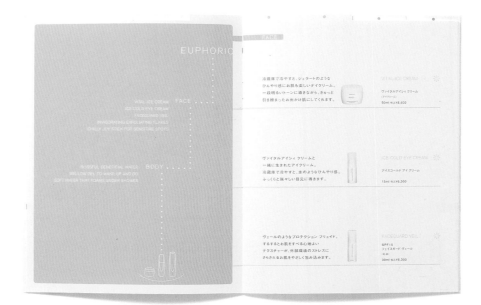

カタログ Catalogue Japan 2007
CL, SB: ケンゾーパルファム　Kenzo Parfums

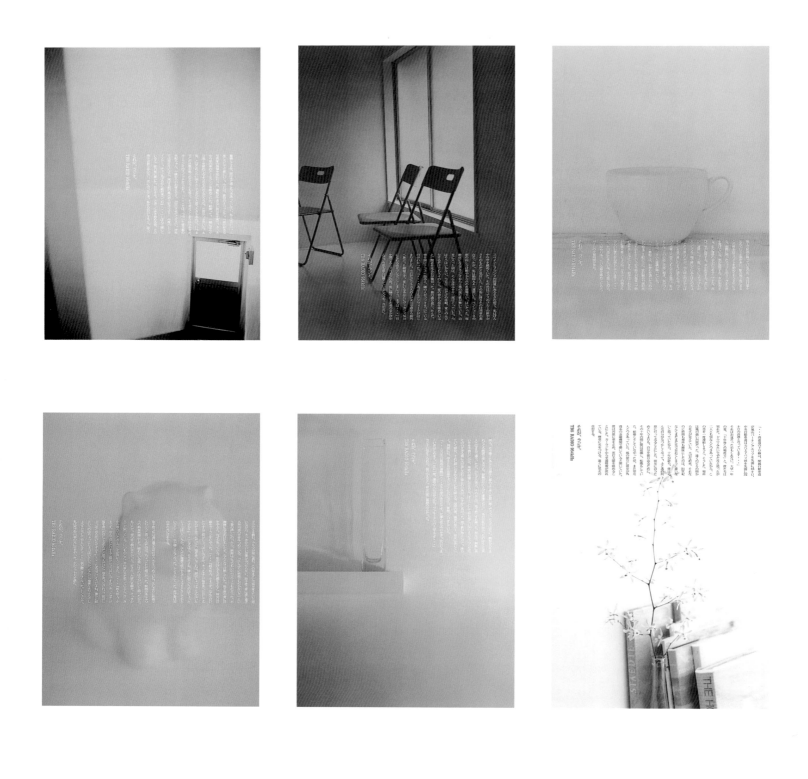

雑誌 **Magazine**　Japan 2005
CL: TBSラジオ＆コミュニケーションズ
　　TBS RADIO & COMMUNICATIONS
CD, AD: 山田 英二　Eiji Yamada
D: 野寺 尚子　Naoko Nodera
P: 泊 昭雄　L.A. Tomari
CW: 高木 基　Moto Takagi
Agency: 電通　DENTSU INC.
DF, SB: ウルトラグラフィックス　ULTRA Graphics

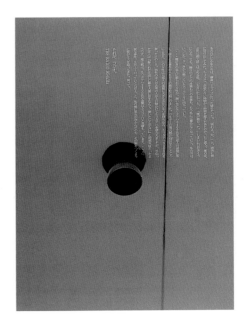

アニュアルレポート Annual Report USA 2004

CL: American Dietetic Association
AD: Tim Hartford
D: Ron Alikpala
P: Ron Wu
SB: Hartford Design

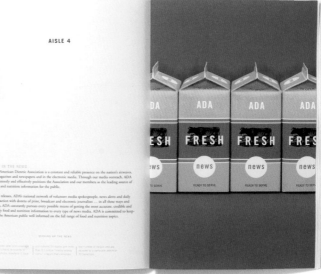

アニュアルレポート **Annual Report** USA 2003

CL: American Dietetic Association
AD, D: Tim Hartford
P: Kipling Swehla
DF, SB: Hartford Design

パッケージ **Package** Japan 2003
CL: 良品計画 RYOHIN KEIKAKU Co., Ltd.
CD: 庵 豊 Yutaka Iori
AD: 新村 則人 Norito Shinmura
D: 庭野 広祐 Kousuke Niwano
P: 藤岡 直樹 Naoki Fujioka
Agency: アイアンドエスビービーディオー I&S/BBDO
DF, SB: 新村デザイン事務所 shinmura design office

ポスター Poster Japan 2004 – 2005
CL: ディノス Dinos Inc.
CD, AD: 水野 学 Manabu Mizuno
D: 上村 昌 Masaru Uemura
P: 瀧本 幹也 Mikiya Takimoto
DF, SB: グッドデザインカンパニー good design company

a

b

active
comfortable.

SPRING 2006

Eddie Bauer

ナノテックス™の生地を採用し汚れを寄せつけない高レベル
の撥水性とストレッチのはきやすい快適性を追求。すっきりと
したストレートシルエットのナノストレッチパンツ。普段のお手
入れが簡単でデイリー・ユースに最適です。

Nano-Tex™ Stretch Pant ¥6,900(税込)
3/4 Sleeve Patterned Wrinkle-Resistant Shirt ¥5,900(税込)
※3月中旬発売予定
Belted Loafer ¥12,900(税込)

Delightful spring color.

3/4 Sleeve Patterned Wrinkle-Resistant Shirt ¥5,900(税込)
※3月中旬発売予定
3/4 Sleeve Wrinkle-Resistant Shirt ¥5,900(税込)
※3月中旬発売予定

c

a　リーフレット　Leaflet
b, c カタログ　Catalogue　Japan　2007 (a, b), 2006 (c)
CL: エディー・バウアー・ジャパン　Eddie Bauer Japan, Inc.
CD, AD, D, SB: サイトヲ ヒデユキ　Hideyuki Saito

a, b, c カタログ Catalogue　Japan　2007 (a), 2005 (b, c)
CL: ビルケンシュトックジャパン BIRKENSTOCK JAPAN Co., Ltd.
CD, AD, D, CW, SB: サイトヲ ヒデユキ Hideyuki Saito
P: 大沼 ショージ Shoji Onuma / 西谷 徹哉 Tetsuya Nishitani
Producer: 遠藤 ひろゆき Hiroyuki Endo

b

c

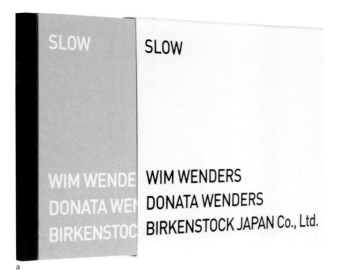

a

b

c

a カタログ Catalogue Japan 2006
CL: ビルケンシュトックジャパン BIRKENSTOCK JAPAN Co., Ltd.
CD, AD, D, SB: サイトヲ ヒデユキ Hideyuki Saito
P: Wim Wenders / Donata Wenders
Producer: 遠藤 ひろゆき Hiroyuki Endo

b パンフレット Pamphlet Japan 2004
CL: ベネッセコーポレーション Benesse Corporation
AD: 松下 計 Kei Matsushita
D: 田辺 智子 Tomoko Tanabe
Agency: 電通 DENTSU INC.
SB: 松下計デザイン室 KEI Matsushita Design Room Inc.

c 書籍 Book Japan 2004
CL: W'ALL
AD: 副田 高行 Takayuki Soeda
D: 貝塚 智子 Tomoko Kaizuka
P: 泊 昭雄 L.A. Tomari
SB: 副田デザイン制作所 SOEDA DESIGN FACTORY

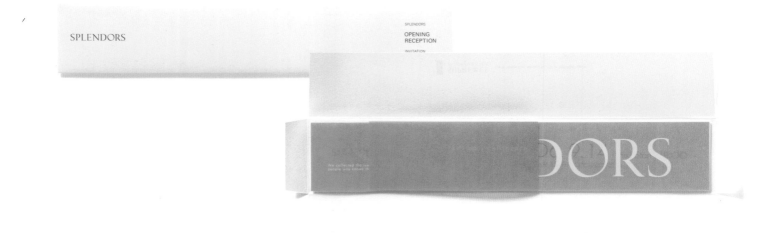

ダイレクトメール　DM　Japan　2006
CL: スープリームス インコーポレーテッド　SUPREMES INCORPORATED
CD: Jet State
AD: 久住 欣也　Yoshinari Hisazumi (HD LAB Inc.)
D: 坂口 智彦　Tomohiko Sakaguchi (HD LAB Inc.)
P: 武田 一枝　Kazue Takeda
CW: 宮崎 真（モノタイプ）　Makoto Miyazaki (MONOTYPE)
DF, SB: HD LAB Inc.

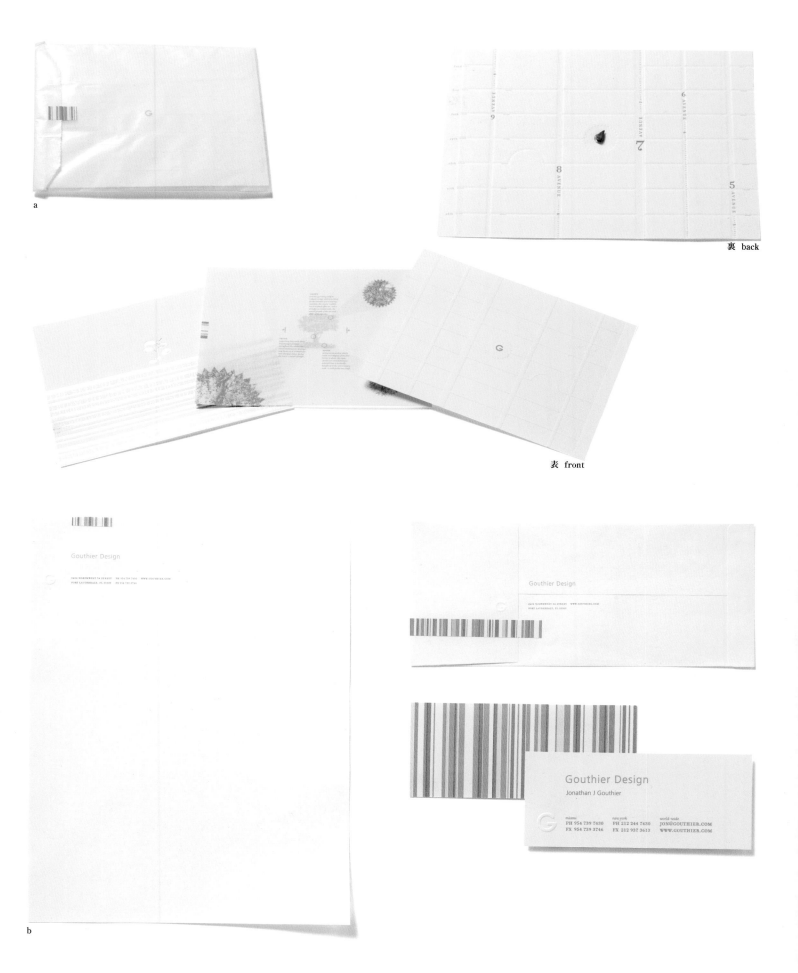

a　裏　back

表　front

a チラシ Flyer
b ステーショナリー Stationery　USA　2007 (a), 2002 (b)
CL, SB: Gouthier Design
DF: Gouthier Design : A Brand Collective

a 装丁 **Book Cover**　Japan　2006
CL: テイクアンドギヴ・ニーズ
　　TAKE and GIVE NEEDS Co., Ltd.
CD, CW: 武藤 雄一　Yuichi Muto
AD, D: 安田 由美子　Yumiko Yasuda
D: 岡崎 智弘　Tomohiro Okazaki
DF, SB: アイルクリエイティブ　ayrcreative

a* ホワイトのしおりは自分の好きな頁に、グレーのしおりは迷った時に
　　読む頁に、エンジのしおりは一番忘れてはいけない頁に使用してもらえる
　　ように3色用意されている
　　Three different colored ribbons have been provided for different uses:
　　white to mark a page the reader fancies, gray to mark a point of reference,
　　and red that which one must not forget.

b ステーショナリー **Stationery**　USA　2006

CL: Desirability
DF: Gouthier Design : A Brand Collective
SB: Gouthier Design

Aqui, debajo del planeo
de los milanos...

El
Milano
Real

Pasear
por
el
pinar

subir a las cumbres de Gredos,

y las orillas del río Tormes,

pasear a caballo
o en bicicleta.

viendo desde los ventanales del comedor

cómo

c

a

e

la nieve,

único

sentarse
a tomar café

frente al mirador
desde
donde
se ve

un
paisaje

O
o

O simplemente
sentarse a ver el paisaje
oyendo solamente
el sonido del viento
en los árboles.

hacer todas estas cosas normales

que en pocos sitios se pueden hacer como aquí.

ブローシャー　Brochure　Spain　2002

CL: El Milano Real
AD, D, I: Gabriel Martinez
AD: Sonia Diaz
DF, SB: LSD

a ブローシャー Brochure　USA　2005

CL: Golden State Vineyards
AD, D: David Schuemann
DF, SB: CF NAPA

b 招待状 Invitation　Italy　2004

CL: Reptile's House
AD: Marco Molteni / Margherita Monguzzi
Agency, DF: jekyll & hyde
SB: Jekyll & Hyde

c

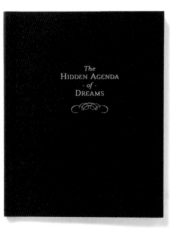

d

c ブローシャー Brochure USA 2005

CL: The Nature Conservancy of California
AD: Dorothy Remington
D: Kern Toy
P: Walt Denson
CW: Linda Peterson
Agency: Peterson Skolnick + Dodge
DF, SB: Alterpop

d 会社案内 Company Brochure USA 2003

CL, DF, SB: Giorgio Davanzo Design
D: Giorgio Davanzo
CW: Gretchen Lauber

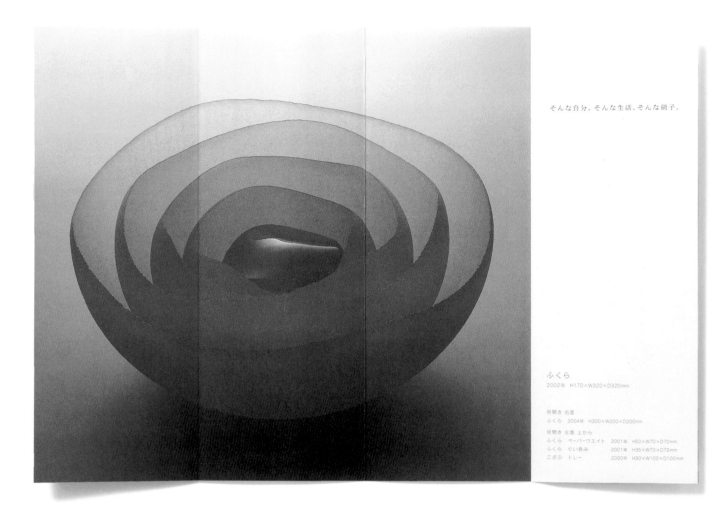

そんな自分。そんな生活。そんな硝子。

ふくら
2002年 H170×W320×D320mm

見開き 右面
ふくら 2004年 H300×W200×D200mm

見開き 左面 上から
ふくら ペーパーウエイト 2001年 H60×W70×D70mm
ふくら ぐい呑み 2001年 H35×W70×D70mm
こざら トレー 2000年 H30×W100×D100mm

小 路 口 力 恵

"小路口屋"
硝子工房

富山県富山市古沢237-3 〒930-0151
Tel.&Fax.076-436-3131
E-mail.shojiguchi_ya@mac.com

b

小 路 口 力 恵

やさしく、やわらかく、ここちよい。

a

a リーフレット Leaflet
b 名刺 Business Card Japan 2006
CL: "小路口屋"硝子工房 "SHOJIGUCHIYA"glass studio
AD, D, SB: 宮田 裕美詠 Yumiyo Miyata
P: 室沢 敏晴 Toshiharu Murosawa
DF: ストライド STRIDE

a

b

c

a ステーショナリー　Stationery
b ショップカード　Shop Card
c ステッカー　Sticker　Mexico　2004

CL: Taller de Empresa
CD, D: Vanessa Eckstein
D: Vanesa Enriques / Mariana Contegni
P: Fernando Cordero
DF, SB: Bløk Design

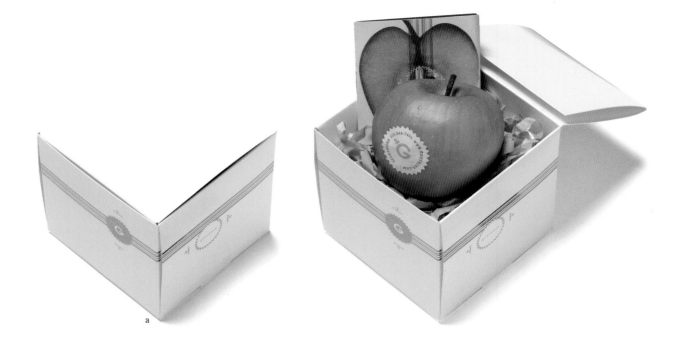

a

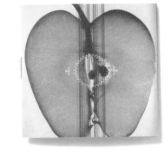

a PRツール PR Tool USA 2007

CL, SB: Gouthier Design
DF: Gouthier Design : A Brand Collective

b アイデンティティーシステム
Identity System UK 2005

CL: Iron Design
AD, D: Jonathan HowellsPaul Garbet
DF, SB: Dinnick & Howells

b

カタログ Catalogue Japan 2007
CL, SB: GINZA TANAGOKORO FATZ Co., Ltd.
CD: 杉田 淳子 Atsuko Sugita (GINZA TANAGOKORO FATZ Co., Ltd.)
AD, D: 山口 拓三 Takuzo Yamaguchi (GAROWA GRAPHICO)
DF: GAROWA GRAPHICO
P: 木下 大造（木下大造写真事務所） Daizou Kinoshita Photographic Office Inc.
CW: 大江 淳一 Jyunichi Oe (GINZA TANAGOKORO FATZ Co., Ltd.)

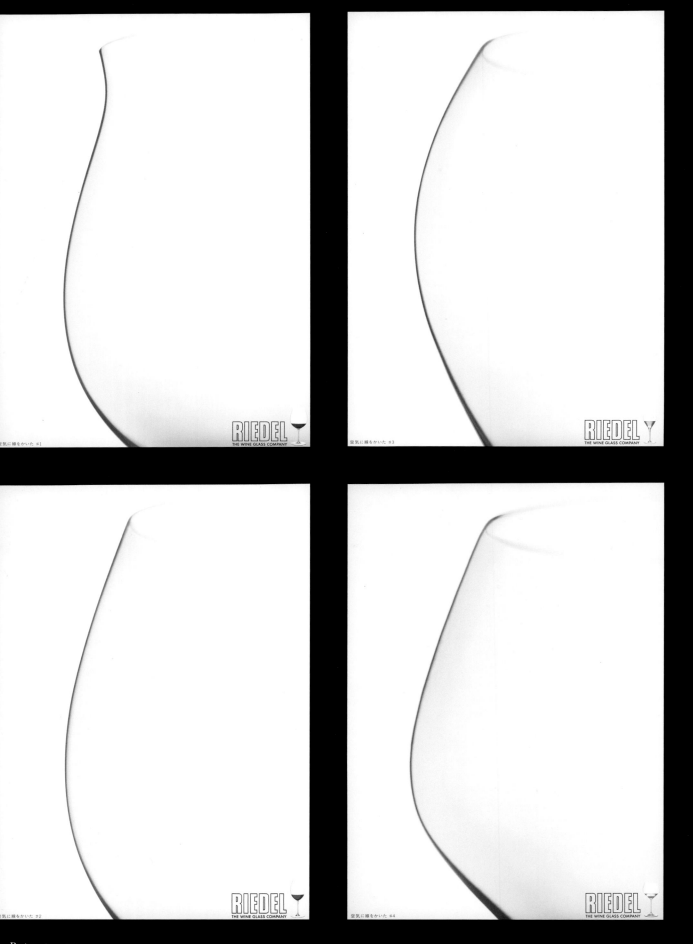

空気に線をかいた #1

RIEDEL
THE WINE GLASS COMPANY

空気に線をかいた #3

RIEDEL
THE WINE GLASS COMPANY

空気に線をかいた #2

RIEDEL
THE WINE GLASS COMPANY

空気に線をかいた #4

RIEDEL
THE WINE GLASS COMPANY

ー Poster　Japan　2007
ーデルジャパン　RIEDEL JAPAN Co., Ltd.
V: 武藤 雄一　Yuichi Muto
安田 由美子　Yumiko Yasuda
智弘　Tomohiro Okazaki
順　Jun Kumagai
アイルクリエイティブ　ayrcreative

ブローシャー **Brochure** Italy 2006
CL, SB: Jekyll & Hyde
CD, AD, D: Marco Molteni / Margherita Monguzzi
CW: Danila Massara
Agency, DF: jekyll & hyde

a

a パッケージ Package
b 招待状 Invitation　Australia　2003 ~ 2004

CL: Nautlis Group
AD: Vince Frost
D: Anthony Donovan / Bridget Atkinson
DF, SB: Frost Design

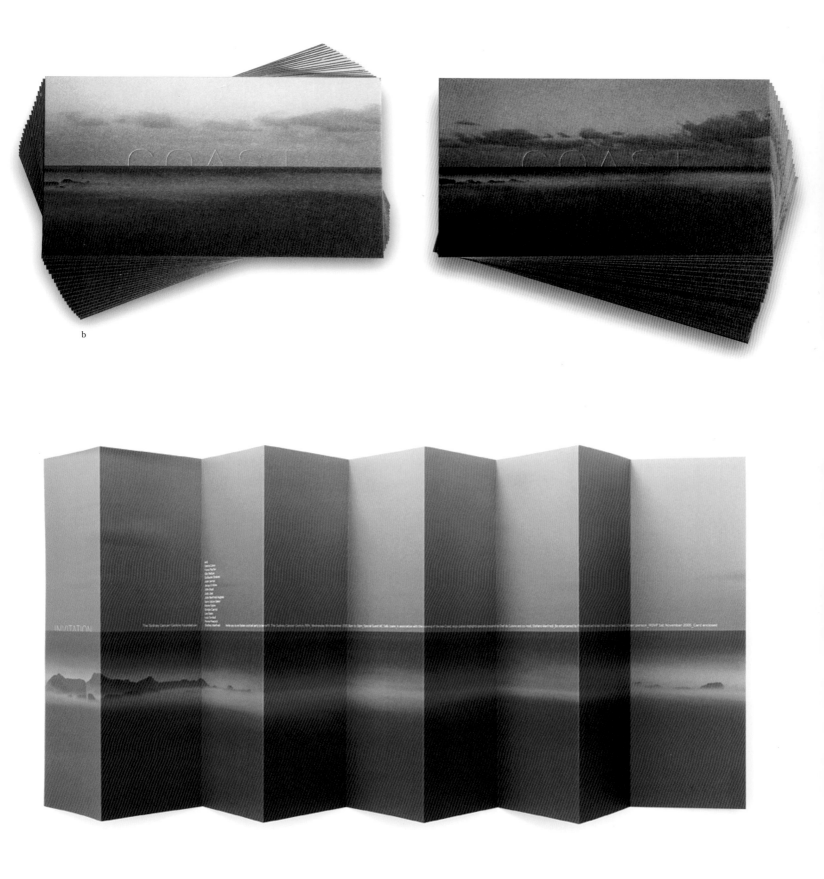

b

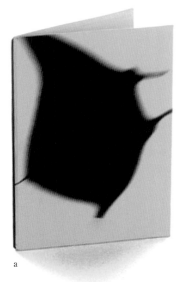

a

dolci

Vanilla buttermilk panna cotta with summer berries | 15
Poached peaches with amaretto flavoured zabaglione | 15
Chocolate and nougat tartufo | 15
Mango and panettone pudding | 15
Tarte dedadore with caramelised fig, mascarpone cream and vincotto | 15
Gelati and sorbetti | 15
Tasting plate of four desserts | 49

cheese

Buche Blanche brignon – white mould, goat's milk, France | 15
Gorgonzola Piccante – blue, cow's milk, Italy | 15
Taleggio washed rind, cow's milk, Italy | 15
Il Mugellane – sheep's and cow's milk, Italy | 15
Tasting of four cheeses | 28

dessert wine

03 Alasia moscato d'asti 750ml Piedmont Italy | 8 | 40
03 Coriole 'Rachel' chenin McLaren Vale SA | 8 | 40
01 McWilliams Reserve botrytis Semillon Riverina NSW | 45
00 Morgan botrytis Semillon Hunter Valley NSW | 50
02 De Bortoli 'Noble One' botrytis Semillon Riverina NSW | 14 | 62
03 Crawford River 'Nektar' botrytis Riesling Condah VIC | 67
NV Veuve Clicquot Demi-Sec Reims, France | 75
86 Chateau De Fargues botrytis Semillon 750ml Sauternes, France | 295

cognac & armagnac

Martell VSOF | 10
Courvoisier VSOF | 11
Les Antiquaries VSOF | 12
Delamain XO | 15
Hennessy XO | 18
Remy Martin XO | 20
Jean Dubroy Vintage | 33

1985 Delord BA | 11
Chateau Tariquet Folle Blanche BA | 15
1985 Domaine du Goudu GBA | 23
1970 Castarède GBA | 29

b

c

a メニュー Menu
b パッケージ Package
c 招待状 Invitation   Australia 2006

CL: Nautlis Group
AD: Vince Frost
D: Anthony Donovan
DF, SB: Frost Design

a ブローシャー Brochure
b パッケージ Package   Australia 2006

CL: Yalumba Wine Company
AD, D: Anntte Harcus
CW: Yalumba
DF, SB: Harcus Design

a

a

b

c

a パッケージ　Package
b メニュー　Menu
c ショップカード　Shop Card　USA　2003

CL: Locanda Vini e Olii Restaurant
AD, D: Matteo Bologna
D: Andrea Brown
DF: Mucca Design Corp.
SB: Mucca Design

a

b

c

a パッケージ Package USA 2006
CL: Facelli Winery
D: Giorgio Davanzo
DF, SB: Giorgio Davanzo Design

b パッケージ Package USA 2006
CL: Precept Brands
D: Giorgio Davanzo
DF, SB: Giorgio Davanzo Design

c パッケージ Package Australia 2006
CL: Il Fornaio
AD: Rainer Bulach
D: Domenic Minieri / Felicity Davison
P: Marcus Struzina
Agency, DF, SB: Hoyne Design

a

The best out of grapes.

R. K. Schmidt, wine dealer
Importer of fine french wines www.weine-vom-nachbarn.de

The best out of grapes.

R. K. Schmidt, wine dealer
Importer of fine french wines www.weine-vom-nachbarn.de

The best out of grapes.

R. K. Schmidt, wine dealer
Importer of fine french wines www.weine-vom-nachbarn.de

a 雑誌 Magazine   Germany 2005
  CL: Weinhandel Rainer K.Sochmidt
  AD: Marco Antonio
  AD, CW: Henning Patzner
  CD Copy: Doerete Spengler - Abrense
  CD Art: Jan Rexhausen
  Agency, SB: Jung von Matt/9

b メニュー Menu   Mexico 2007
  CL: Ödün
  CD: Vanessa Eckstein
  D: Mariana Contegni / Patricia Kleebers
  DF, SB: Bløk Design

c ダイレクトメール DM   UK 2006
  CL, DF, SB: HAT-TRICK DESIGN
  AD: Jim Sutuerland / David kimpton / Greatnowat
  D: Ben Christie

b

c

Galera. sólo cocinas bulthaup. Jorge Juan, 17 28001 Madrid Tel. 91 435 05 15 Fax 91 781 05 74 e-mail: galerav@infonegocio.com

Galera sólo bulthaup

ポスター Poster Spain 2003 ~ 2005
CL, D: Gabriel Martines
AD: Paz Martin
P: Gigaphoto: Juan F Seoane y Salvador Gonzalez
CW: Frank Memelsdrpff
Agency: GMI
DF, SB: LSD

a

b

a 案内状 Moving Card Italy 2002
CL, AD, SB: Adriana Brunetti
AD: Sandra Holt

b ダイレクトメール DM Japan 2007
CL: トラットリア・ブリッコラ TRATTORIA Briccola
CD, AD: 松下 計 Kei Matsushita
D: 渡辺 京子 Kyoko Watanabe
SB: 松下計デザイン室 KEI Matsushita Design Room Inc.

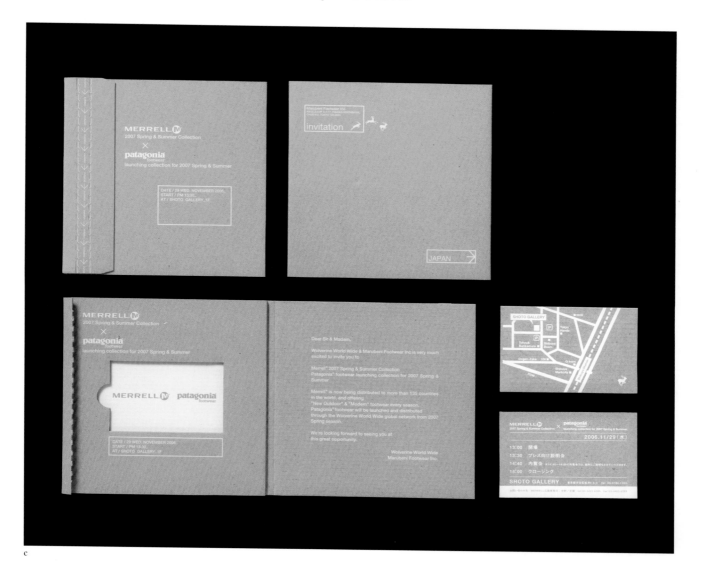

c

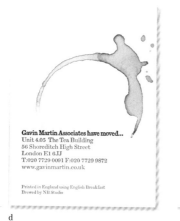   

d

c ダイレクトメール　DM　Japan 2006
CL: 丸紅フットウェア　MARUBENI FOOTWEAR Inc.
AD, D: 中島 裕治　Yuji Nakajima
CW: 追川 知紀　Tomonori Oikawa
DF, SB: 博報堂プロダクツ　HAKUHODO PRODUCT'S

d 案内状　Moving Card　UK 2002
CL: Gavin Martin Associates
AD: Ben Stott / Alan Dye / Nick Finney
D, CW: Alan Dye
SB: NB Studio

a

b

c

a ショップ Shop
b パッケージ Package
c ショップバッグ Shop Bag UK 2002 - 2007

CL: EAT
AD: Angus Hyland
DF, SB: Pentagram

a ショップバッグ Shop bag
b カップ Cup
c エプロン Apron
d T-シャツ T-shirt　Great Britain　2006

CL: IQBAL WAHAB
AD, I: Pierre Vermeir
D, I: Tommy Taylor
I: Aaron Shaw
DF, SB: HGV

はじめてのベッドシーン。

「優しい子に育ってほしい、人にも地球にも。」

ペットボトルから、ペットボトルが生まれる。

ペットボトルのリサイクル製品に
待望のニューフェイス誕生!!
ペットボトルをもとのペットボトルに再生し、
半永久的に続くリサイクルの輪を完成させる
「完全循環型ペットボトル」です。
期待を一身に背負ったペットボトルの子供たち、
ずっと大切に育てていこうと思います。

すべてのペットボトルに
新しい命を授けたい、サントリーです。

SUNTORY

b

b 雑誌広告 Magazine Ad Japan 2005

a ポスター Poster Japan 2004

CL: アップリカ葛西 Aprica Kasai Inc.
CD: 葛西 康人 Yasuhito Kasai / 宇和川 泰道 Yasumichi Uwagawa
AD: 立石 義博 Yoshihiro Tateishi / 吉川 努 Tsutomu Yoshikawa
D: 木村 真也 Shinya Kimura / 濱田 麻梨子 Mariko Hamada
P: 上田 義彦 Yoshihiko Ueda
CW: 鈴木 勝 Msaru Suzuki / 香西 伸子 Nobuko Kozai
DF: サブライム Sublime Inc.
Printing Director: 岩垣 平 Osamu Iwagaki / 二字 奈穂美 Naomi Niji
Agency, SB: 電通 関西支社「TOKYO ROOM」 DENTSU INC. KANSAI

CL: サントリー SUNTORY LTD.
CD: 加藤 英夫 Hideo Kato
CD, CW: 西脇 淳 Jun Nishiwaki
AD: 喜多 真二 Shinji Kita / 岡 大緑 Dairoku Oka
D: 中村 元 Hajime Nakamura
P: 佐藤 孝仁 Takahito Sato
Creative Producer: 平野 巨実子 Kimiko Hirano
Stylist: 岡村 雅人 Masato Okamura
Art: 北川 治 Osamu Kitagawa
DF: 大広 クリエイティブ＆パートナーズ DAIKO CREATIVE AND PARTNERS INC.
Agency, SB: 大広 DAIKO ADVERTISING INC.

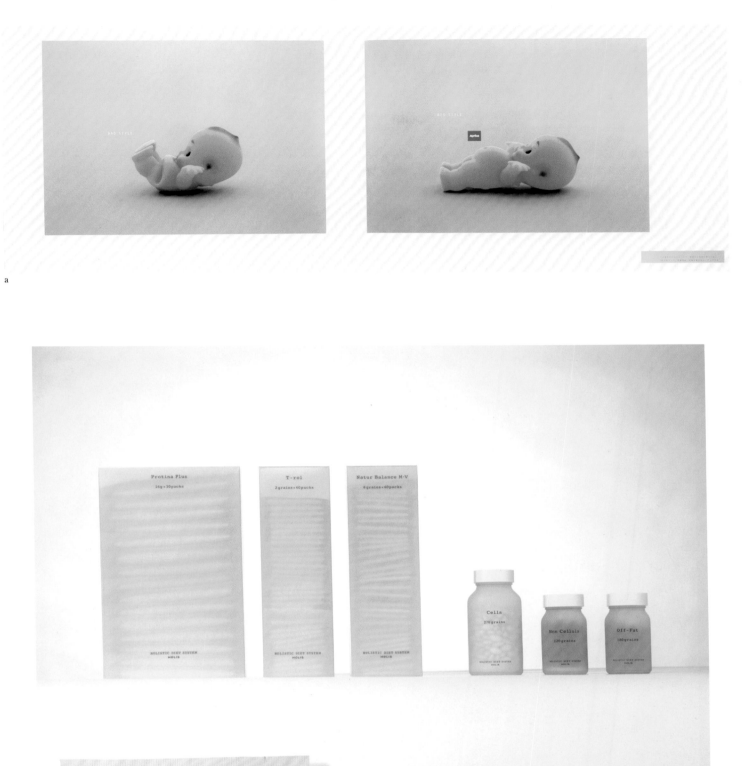

a

c

c パッケージ Package   Japan   2003

CL: フェスタ FESTA Co., Ltd.
CD: 李 和淑 Lee Hwa Suk
AD: 池田 泰幸 Yasuyuki Ikeda / 石井 洋二 Yoji Ishii
D: 引地 摩里子 Mariko Hikichi / 清水 佳代子 kayoko Shimizu
DF, SB: サン・アド SUN-AD CO., LTD.

LET'S WORK OUT AND KEEP YOUR BODY MOVING,
IT'S AS NATURAL AS A BIRD TO FLY

ENJOY SUNSHINE AND FEEL THE FORCE OF **NATURE**, DON'T HIDE
Think and act naturally, it's the way for A HEALTHY LIFE

ポスター　Poster　Taiwan　2006

CL: Taiwan International Poster Design Awards
AD, D: William Ho Siu Chuen / Chinlee Ma
D: Eddy Chun
DF, SB: HIPPO STUDIO

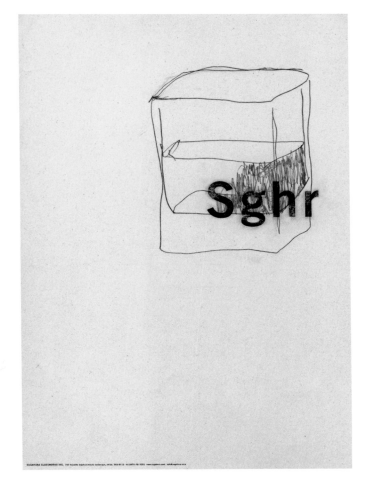

ポスター Poster Japan 2004
CL: 菅原工芸硝子 Sugahara Glassworks Inc.
AD, D: 居山 浩二 Koji Iyama
DF, SB: イヤマデザイン iyamadesign

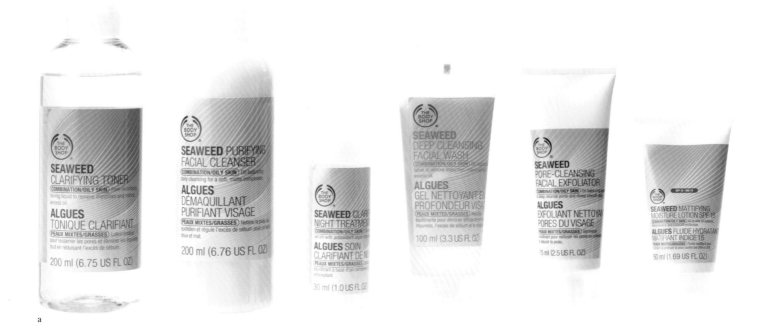

a

c

a, b パッケージ Package Japan 2006 (b), 2007 (a)
　　CL, SB: ザ・ボディショップ THE BODY SHOP

c パッケージ Package Canada 2006
　　CL: ICC
　　CD, D: Vanessa Eckstein
　　AD: Marc Stoiber (Change)
　　D: Mariana Contegni
　　I: Brian Rea
　　Agency: Change
　　DF, SB: Bløk Design

d カタログ Catalogue Italy 2007
　　CL: DeRoma group
　　AD: Joseph Rossi
　　D, Agency: GraphicFirstAid
　　P: Edith Andreotta / Giuliano Francesconi
　　Agency, SB: joseph rossi

b

d

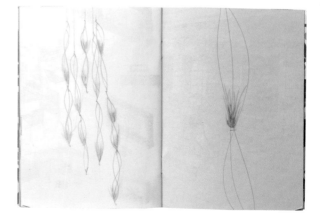

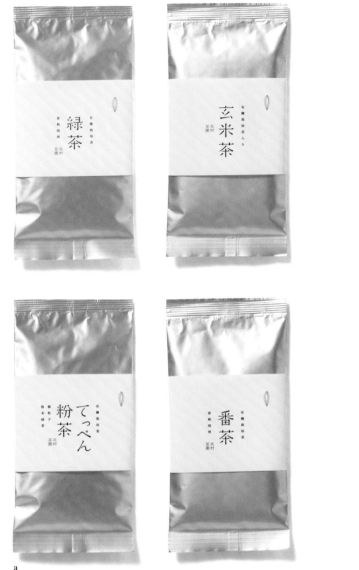

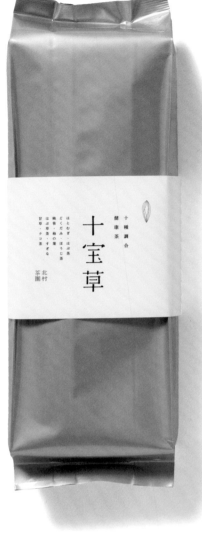

a

b

a パッケージ Package　Japan 2003

　CL: キャップフォーメーション CAP FORMATION Co., Ltd.
　AD, D: 古賀 義孝　Yoshitaka Koga
　AD: 小松 大介　Daisuke Komatsu
　SB: 井手写真製版 IDE SHASHINSEIHAN

b パッケージ Package　Japan 2007

　CL, SB: 丸八製茶場 maruhachiseichajyo
　D: スズキ タクミ　Takumi Suzuki

c ペーパーバッグ Paper Bag
d ショップ カード Shop Card
e 名刺 Business Card　Japan 2004

　CL: 漢方専門薬局「環」Tamaki
　AD: 美澤 修　Osamu Misawa
　D: 梶谷 聡美　Satomi Kajitani
　SB: 美澤修デザイン室 osamu misawa designroom Co., Ltd.

f PR紙 PR Magazine　Japan 2006

　CL: 高知県　Kochi Prefecture
　CD, AD, D: 梅原 真　Makoto Umebara
　DF, SB: 梅原デザイン事務所 Umebara Design Office

c

d

e

f

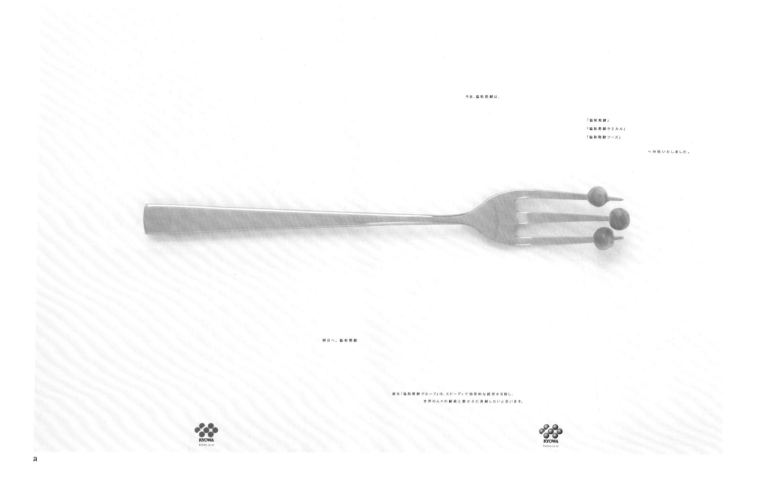

今日、協和発酵は。

「協和発酵」
「協和発酵ケミカル」
「協和発酵フーズ」

へ分社いたしました。

明日へ、協和発酵

新生「協和発酵グループ」は、スピーディで効率的な経営を目指し、
世界の人々の健康と豊かさに貢献したいと思います。

a

a 新聞広告 Newspaper Ad Japan 2005
CL: 協和発酵 KYOWA HAKKO Co., Ltd.
CD: 新妻 英信 Hidenobu Nizuma
AD: 森本 千絵 Chie Morimoto
D: 長澤 弘浩 Hiromasa Nagasawa / 細川 剛 Go Hosokawa
　 内田 善基 Yoshiki Uchida / 近田 智之 Tomoyuki Chikada
P: 泊 昭雄 Akio Tomari
CW: 曽原 剛 Go Sohara
SB: 博報堂クリエイティブヴォックス
　 HAKUHODO CREATIVE VOX Inc.

b

b パッケージ Package Japan 2003
CL: 小豆島ヘルシーランド Shodoshima Healthyland Co., Ltd.
CD, AD, D: 左合 ひとみ Hitomi Sago
DF, SB: 左合ひとみデザイン室 Hitomi Sago Desin Office

生まれた国の、
野菜を食べよう。

ゆうき畑

舌は欧米化されても、
体は日本人です。

ゆうき畑

美しい野菜ほど、
危険かもしれない。

ゆうき畑

a

a パッケージ Package   Japan 2004

CL, SB: キリンビール Kirin Brewery Co., Ltd.
CD: 守屋 祐亮 Yusuke Moriya
AD: 牧野 正文 Masafumi Makino

b パッケージ Package
c はがき Post Card
d ポスター Poster   Japan 2006

CL: 濱川商店 Hamakawa Brewery Co., Ltd.
CD, AD, D: はちうま みほこ Mihoko Hachiuma
P: 河上 展儀 Nobuyosih Kawakami
CW: 池田 あけみ Akemi Ikeda
SB: オフィス・エム Office, m

b

c

|bijofu schwa|

|bijofu schwa|

その酒、しゅわと来ませり。

|bijofu schwa|

発泡吟醸酒 [美丈夫しゅわっ!!]

d

ブローシャー **Brochure** Italy 2006

CL: P&G Prestige Products
AD: Mario Rullo / Mario Fois
D: Simone Peccedi
Agency, DF: Vertigo Design
SB: Vertigo Design s.r.l.

Simple Sweet

カレンダー　Calendar　Japan　2004
CL: ワコール　Wacoal Corp.
CD: 延井 祐子　Yuko Nobui
AD: 前田 義生　Yoshio Maeda
D: 寺村 直子　Naoko Teramura
I: 末岡 美穂子　Mihoko Sueoka
Agency: 凸版印刷　TOPPAN PRINTING Co., Ltd.
DF, SB: スクーデリア　scuderia inc.

Lacy Beauty

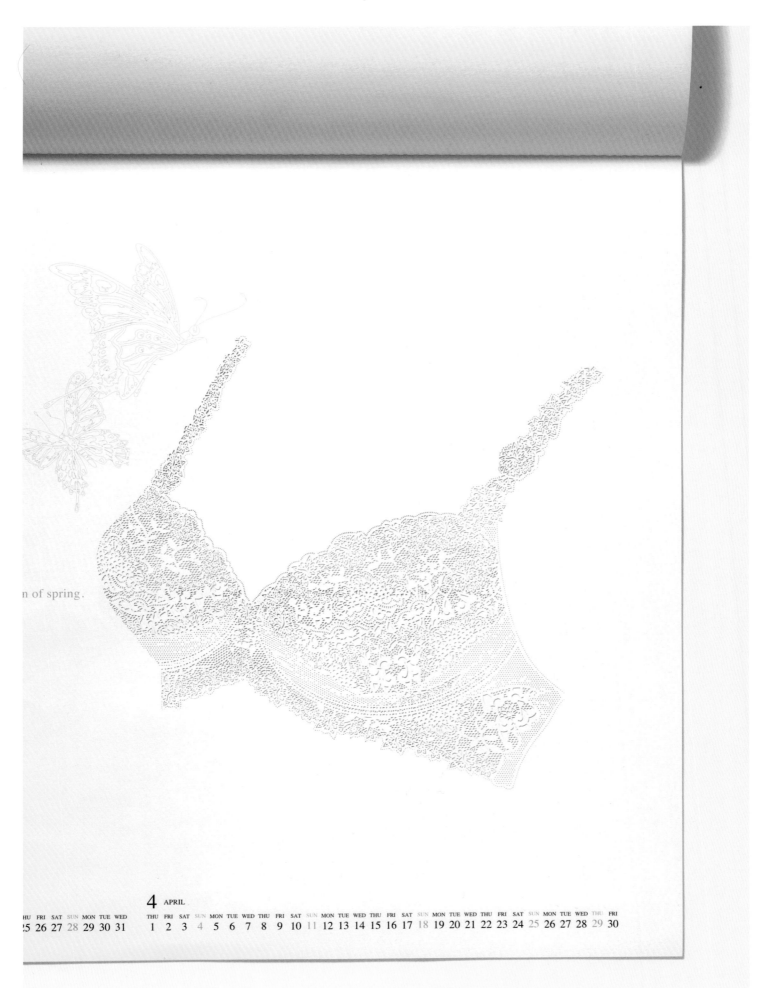

...n of spring.

4 APRIL

THU	FRI	SAT	SUN	MON	TUE	WED	THU	FRI	SAT	SUN	MON	TUE	WED	THU	FRI	SAT	SUN	MON	TUE	WED	THU	FRI	SAT	SUN	MON	TUE	WED	THU	FRI
25	26	27	28	29	30	31	1	2	3	4	5	6	7	8	9	10	11	12	13	14	15	16	17	18	19	20	21	22	23	24	25	26	27	28	29	30

a

b

a ポスター　Poster　Japan 2003
CL: 花曜の会　Kayou no Kai
CD: 高橋 修宏　Nobuhiro Takahashi
AD, D: 伊藤 久恵　Hisae Ito
DF, SB: クロス　CROSS Inc.

b ポスター　Poster　Japan 2003
CL: アミューズ　AMUSE Inc.
CD: 横澤 宏一郎　Koichiro Yokozawa
CD, AD: 丹野 英之　Hideyuki Tanno
D: 畑澤 里香　Rika Hatazawa
Agency, SB: 博報堂　HAKUHODO Inc.
DF: ツインズ　Twins

c 作品集　Work Book　Japan 2006
CL, DF: ストライド　STRIDE
AD, D, I, SB: 宮田 裕美詠　Yumiyo Miyata

Miyata
Yumi
yo

c

ポスター Poster Japan 2004

CL: ユナイテッドアローズ UNITED ARROWS LTD.
AD: 葛西 薫 Kaoru Kasai
D: 宮崎 史 Fumi Miyazaki
CW: 一倉 宏 Hiroshi Ichikura
DF, SB: サン・アド SUN-AD CO., LTD.

新しい扉を開けるのが好きだ

私の靴はときどき歌うことがある　　　はい　いいえ
ペンギンを飼ってみたい　　　　　　　はい　いいえ
みずいろのくだものをたべたい　　　　はい　いいえ
雨が降っても怒らない　　　　　　　　はい　いいえ
寝るまえに本を読む　　　　　　　　　はい　いいえ
オーロラの写真を撮りたい　　　　　　はい　いいえ
小学1年隣の席の子をおぼえている　　はい　いいえ
朝の公園に着ていく色がある　　　　　はい　いいえ
眠るときは耳を閉じる　　　　　　　　はい　いいえ
ものを捨てるときチクリとする　　　　はい　いいえ
ひとりで映画にいきたい　　　　　　　はい　いいえ
かっこわるいものは信じない　　　　　はい　いいえ
カリブやケルトの音楽にひかれる　　　はい　いいえ
空の青さをアートだと思う　　　　　　はい　いいえ
イルカの意見を聞いてみたい　　　　　はい　いいえ
目が覚めるまで手をつないでいたい　　はい　いいえ
シンプルなサラダはおいしい　　　　　はい　いいえ
一目惚れして買いものをしたい　　　　はい　いいえ
できるだけ長生きしたい　　　　　　　はい　いいえ
好き嫌いははっきりしている　　　　　はい　いいえ
そういう自分が好きだ　　　　　　　　はい　いいえ
新しい扉を開けるのが好きだ　　　　　はい　いいえ

united arrows
green label relaxing

グリーンレーベル リラクシング 新宿三越店 10月30日オープン
ユナイテッドアローズから生まれた洋服と雑貨のお店です。

160-0455 東京都新宿区新宿3-29-1 新宿三越3F　TEL 03-5363-9760　営業時間 10:00〜20:00

17才

少女は　あいまいなやさしさを嘘だと思った
少年は　線路の向こうの雲以外はくだらないと思った

22才

彼女は　愛ということばを使わないで人生を考えてみた
彼には　あきらめるものさえまだ見つかっていなかった

25才

出会わないのかこのまま　泣くことは怖くないのに
どこまで僕はいけるのか　くりかえす単純なこのビート

28才

笑顔を着ることに慣れすぎている　風の島にいきたい
もうすこし僕は僕であるべきだと　このごろ夕焼けに思う

30才

ありがとう　あなたが貸してくれた音楽が私はすき
わるかった　この仕事が終わったらきっと見つけるから

33才

正直にいえば　外国に行くと帰りたくなくなってしまう
突然いうけど　僕たちは結婚すべきだと思う

united arrows
green label relaxing

グリーンレーベル リラクシング 仙台店 エスパル2階に10月7日オープン
ユナイテッドアローズから生まれた洋服と雑貨のお店です。

980-6977 宮城県仙台市青葉区中央1-1-1 エスパル仙台店2F　TEL 022-256-2302　営業時間 10:00〜20:30

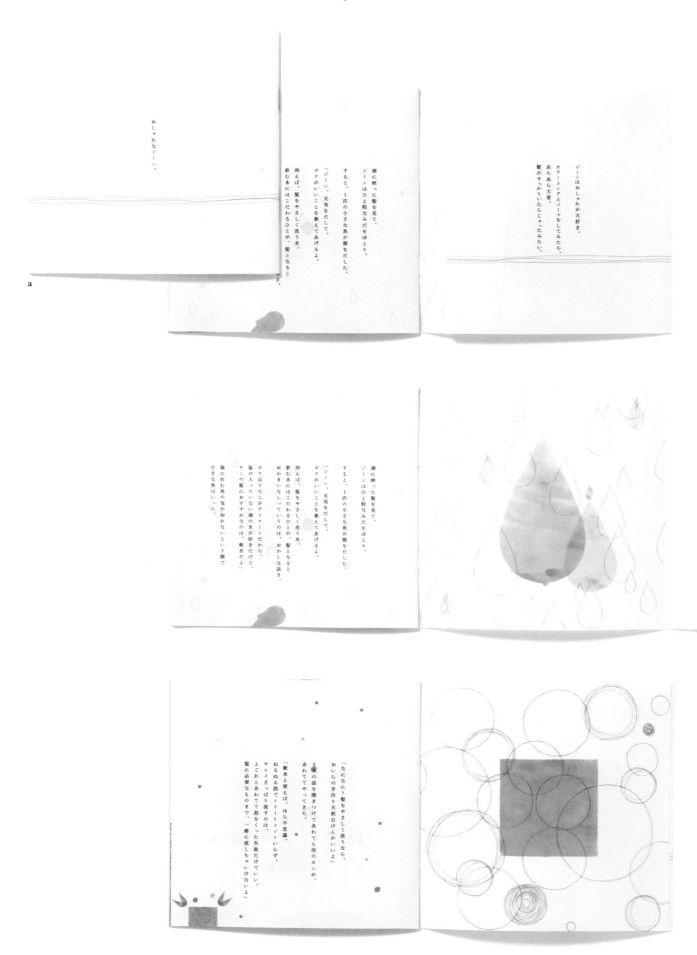

ジーンはおしゃれが大好き。
カラーリングとパーマをしてみたら、
あらあら大変。
髪がすっかりいたんじゃったみたい。

湖に映った髪を見て、
ジーンはひと粒なみだをぼとり。
すると、1匹の小さな魚が顔をだした。
「ジーン、元気をだして。
ボクがいいことを教えてあげるよ。
例えば、髪をやさしく洗う水。
飲む水にはこだわるひとが、髪となると

おしゃれなジーン。

湖に映った髪を見て、
ジーンはひと粒なみだをぼとり。
すると、1匹の小さな魚が顔をだした。
「ジーン、元気をだして。
ボクがいいことを教えてあげるよ。
例えば、髪をやさしく洗う水。
飲む水にはこだわるひとが、髪となると
おかまいなしっていうのは、おかしな話さ。
ボクはうろこがデリケートだから、
塩の入っていない湖の水が好きだけど、
キミの髪におすすめなのは、軟水だよ」
海に住む魚の気が知れないという顔で
小さな魚はいった。

「なになに？髪をやさしく洗うなら、
おいらの手作り天然石けんがいいよ」
2匹の話を聞きつけてあわてん坊のカニが、
あわててやってきた。
「軟水と使えば、ほら不思議。
ぬるぬる泡でトリートメントいらず、
キレイさっぱり流すのは、
よごれとあわてて泡をくった失敗だけでいい。
髪に必要なものまで、一緒に流しちゃいけないよ」

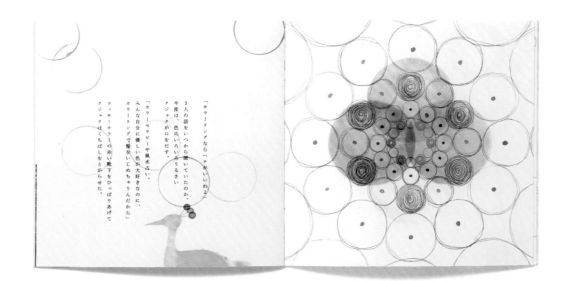

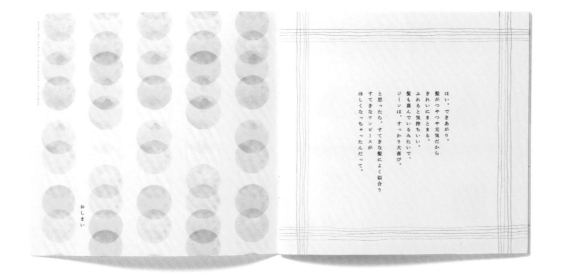

a リーフレット Leaflet
b ポスター Poster Japan 2006
CL: ヘアー・ジーン HAIR GENE
CD, AD, D, P, I: 関 宙明 Hiroaki Seki
CW: フジタノリコ NorikoFujita
DF, SB: ミスター・ユニバース Mr. Universe

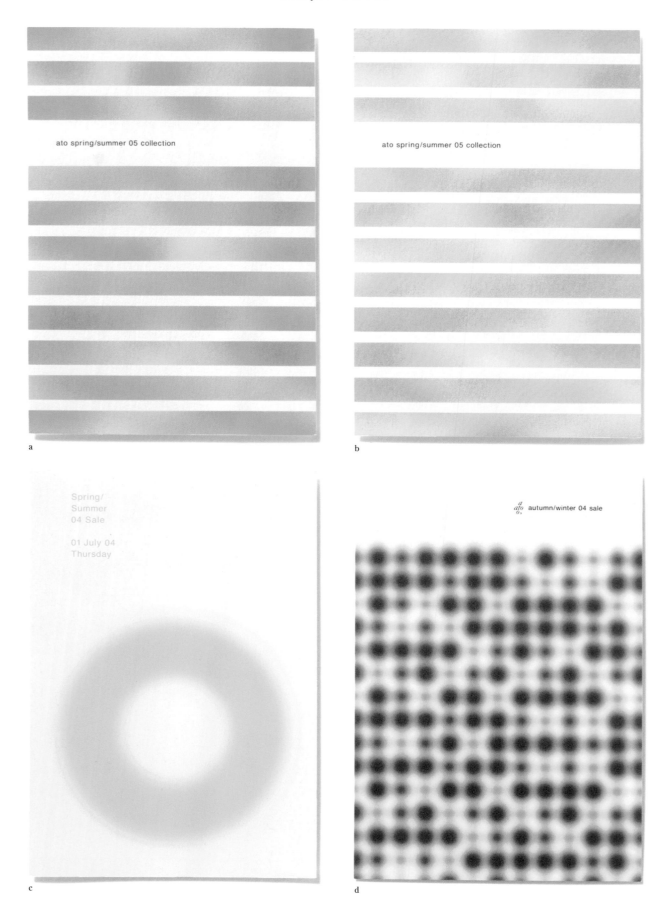

a

ato spring/summer 05 collection

b

ato spring/summer 05 collection

c

Spring/
Summer
04 Sale

01 July 04
Thursday

d

autumn/winter 04 sale

ダイレクトメール DM　Japan　2005 (a, b), 2004 (c, d)
CL: アトウ　ato
AD, D: 草谷 隆文　Takafumi Kusagaya
D: 金坂 義之　Yoshiyuki Kanesaka
DF, SB: 草谷デザイン　Kusagaya Design Inc.

王子じゃ
なくて
おやじ
でもいい

まだ
出会っていない人は、
幸せが
待っている人です。
（結婚を考える委員会）

王子じゃ
なくて
おやじ
でもいい

まだ
出会っていない人は、
幸せが
待っている人です。
（結婚を考える委員会）

王子じゃ
なくて
おやじ
でもいい

まだ
出会っていない人は、
幸せが
待っている人です。
（結婚を考える委員会）

王子じゃ
なくて
おやじ
でもいい

まだ
出会っていない人は、
幸せが
待っている人です。
（結婚を考える委員会）

装丁 Book Cover Japan 2004
CL: ツヴァイ ZWEI Co., Ltd.
CD, CW: 岩崎 俊一 Syunichi Iwasaki
CD, AD, D: 斉藤 順一 Junichi Saito
D: 垂井 洋子 Yoko Tarui
P: 市橋 織江 Orie Ichihashi
CW: 広瀬 純子 Junko Hirose / 岡本 欣也 Kinya Okamoto / 岩崎 亜矢 Aya Iwasaki
Agency: アサツーディ・ケイ ASATSU-DK Inc.
DF, SB: 斎藤デザイン SAITO DESIGN

資生堂会社案内

SHISEIDO
GINZA TOKYO

いつでも、だれでも、どこの場所にいても、

美しく生きることができるように。

日々のみずみずしさにふれ、生きている輝きを感じられるように。

私たち資生堂は、人を幸せにする企業でありたい、と考えています。

美しさと、健やかさ。そのかけがえのない宝物を、

すべての人がわかちあえるように、

化粧品をはじめ、医薬品、トイレタリー製品、食品など

多彩な事業を通じて持てる力のすべてを尽くし、

世の中へ新しい価値をお届けします。

人に喜びをあたえ、豊かな社会を変えることにつながるように

資生堂はこれからも前へ進んでいきます。

海外戦略

多様な肌にあわせ
多彩な文化を尊び、
グローバルブランド「SHISEIDO」を
築き上げてきました。

社会とともに

社会のお役に立つように。
お客さまの生きる喜びに
応えられるように。
資生堂は、社会のよりよき一員として
惜しみなく力を尽くします。

1. 環境への取り組み

会社案内 Company Brochure Japan 2004
CL: 資生堂 SHISEIDO CO., LTD.
CD: 安原 和夫 Kazuo Yasuhara
AD, D: 新村 則人 Norito Shinmura
D, I: 渡辺 由佳 Yuka Watanabe
P: 中村 成一 Seiichi Nakamura
DF, SB: 新村デザイン事務所 shinmura design office

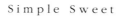

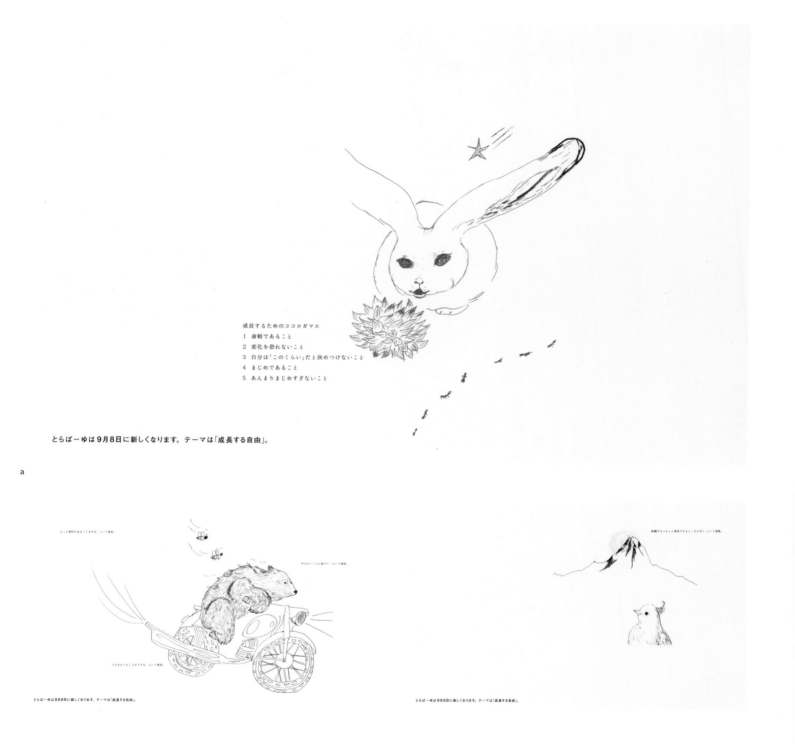

成長するためのココロガマエ
1 身軽であること
2 変化を恐れないこと
3 自分は「このくらい」だと決めつけないこと
4 まじめであること
5 あんまりまじめすぎないこと

とらばーゆは9月8日に新しくなります。テーマは「成長する自由」。

a

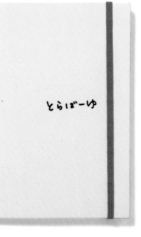

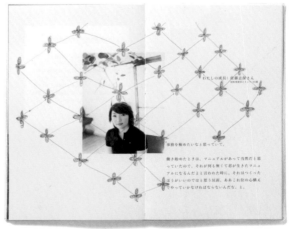

b

a 雑誌広告 Magazine Ad
b リーフレット Leaflet　Japan 2004

CL: リクルート　RECRUIT CO., LTD.
CD: 佐藤 澄子 Sumiko Sato / 米村 浩 Hiroshi Yonemura
AD, D: 坂 哲二 Tetsuji Ban
I: 菅野 旋 Sen Kanno
Agency: ワイデン＋ケネディ トウキョウ Wieden+Kennedy Tokyo
DF, SB: バンデザイン BANG! Design Inc.

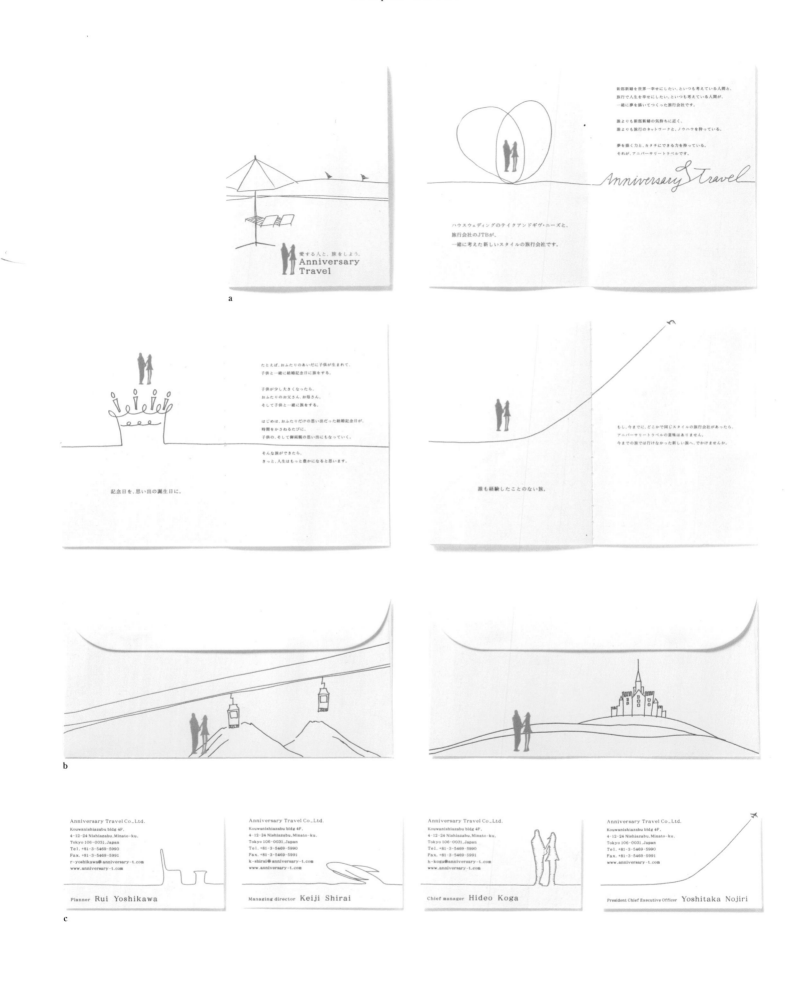

d

a パンフレット Pamphlet
b ステーショナリー Stationery
c 名刺 Business Card   Japan 2006
  CL: アニバーサリートラベル Anniversary Travel
  CD, CW: 武藤 雄一 Yuichi Muto
  AD, D, I: 安田 由美子 Yumiko Yasuda
  I: 藤岡 香織 Kaori Fujioka
  DF, SB: アイルクリエイティブ ayrcreative

d 会社案内 Company Brochure   Japan 2005
  CL, Agency, SB: 日本経済広告社 NIHON KEIZAI ADVERTISING Co., Ltd.
  CD: 中村 方彦 Masahiko Nakamura
  AD, D: 横貫 達巳 Tastumi Yokonuki
  CW: 横山 慶太 Keita Yokoyama
  DF: 日経クリエイティブセンター Nikkei Creative Center, Inc.

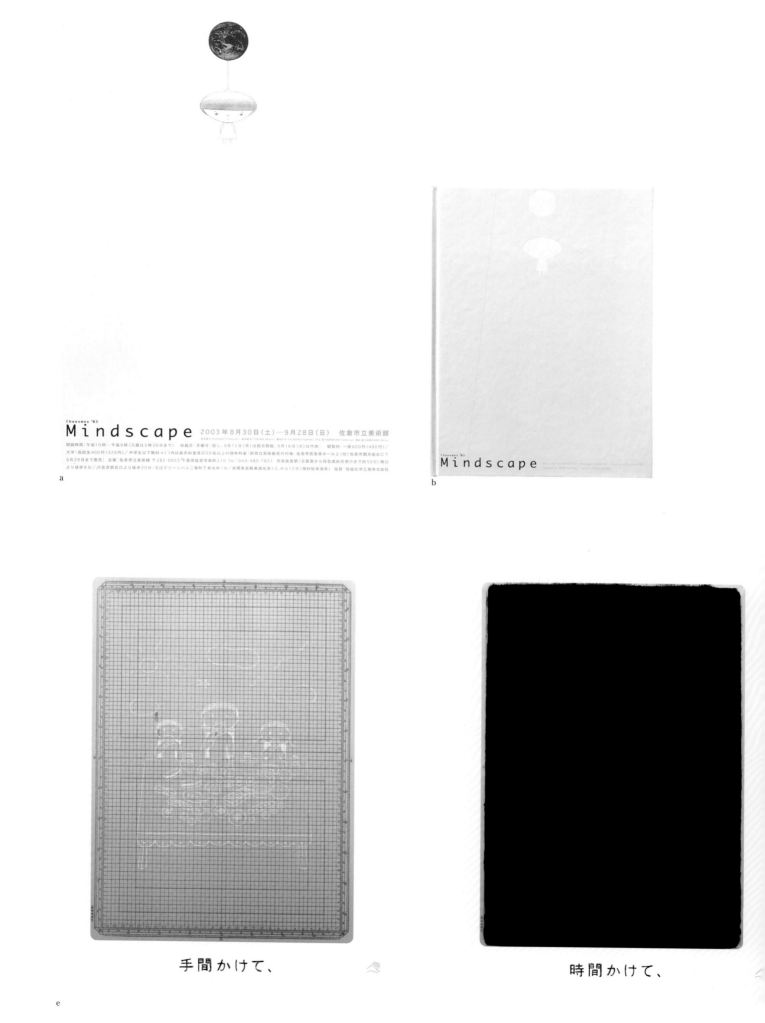

a

b

手間かけて、

時間かけて、

e

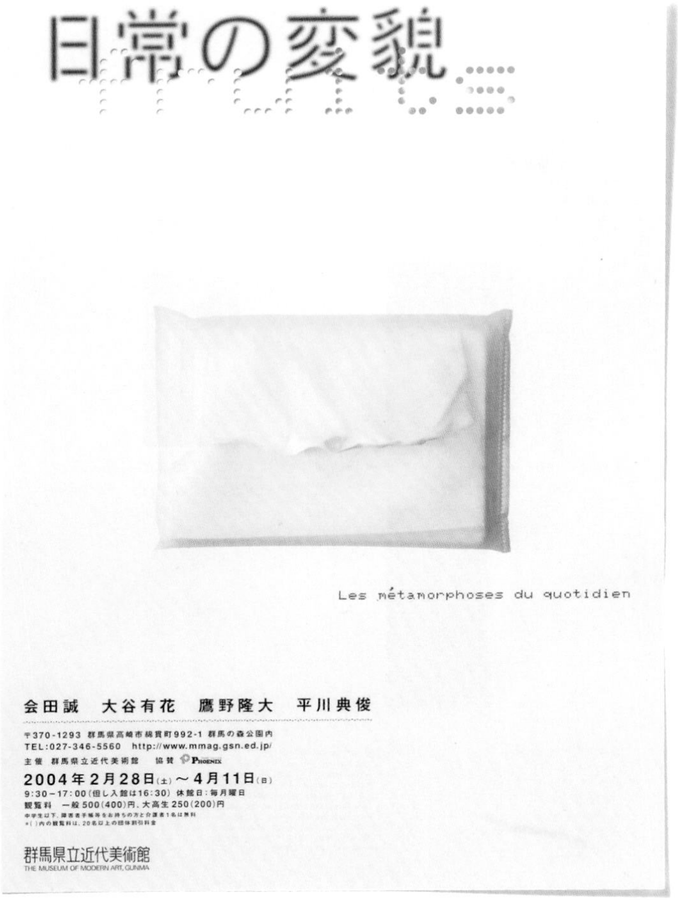
日常の変貌
Les métamorphoses du quotidien
会田誠　大谷有花　鷹野隆大　平川典俊
〒370-1293 群馬県高崎市綿貫町992-1 群馬の森公園内
TEL:027-346-5560　http://www.mmag.gsn.ed.jp/
主催 群馬県立近代美術館　協賛 PHOENIX
2004年2月28日(土)～4月11日(日)
9:30－17:00(但し入館は16:30) 休館日：毎月曜日
観覧料　一般500(400)円、大高生250(200)円
中学生以下、障害者手帳等をお持ちの方と介護者1名は無料
*( )内の観覧料は、20名以上の団体割引料金
群馬県立近代美術館
THE MUSEUM OF MODERN ART, GUNMA

c

日常の変貌
Les métamorphoses du quotidien
群馬県立近代美術館
THE MUSEUM OF MODERN ART, GUNMA

d

できあがり。
手づくりパン
大地の実

a ポスター　Poster
b カタログ　Catalogue　Japan　2003

CL: 佐倉市立美術館　Sakura City Museum of Art
AD, D, SB: 工藤 強勝　Tsuyokatsu Kudo
D: 伊藤 滋章　Shigeaki Ito
I: 藤城 凡子　Namiko Fujishiro (a)
CW: 黒川 公二　Koji Kurokawa
DF: デザイン実験室　Design Laboratory

c パンフレット　Pamphlet
d ダイレクトメール　DM　Japan　2004

CL: 群馬県立近代美術館　The Museum of Modern Art. Gunma
AD: 永井 裕明　Hiroaki Nagai
D: 栗原 幸治　Koji Kurihara
P: 鷹野 隆大　Ryudai Takano
DF, SB: エヌ・ジー　N.G. Inc.

e ポスター　Poster　Japan　2004

CL: 大地の実　Home made bakery "The fruit of the ground"
CD, CW: 武藤 雄一　Yuichi Muto
AD, D, I: 安田 由美子　Yumiko Yasuda
P: 熊谷 順　Jun Kumagai
DF, SB: アイルクリエイティブ　ayrcreative

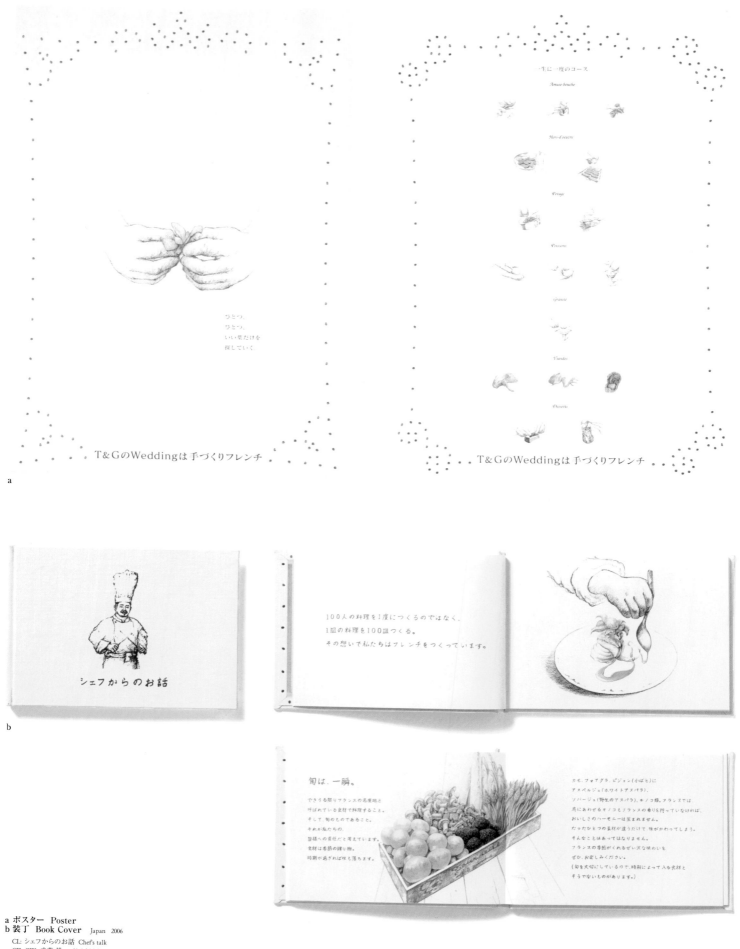

a ポスター Poster
b 装丁 Book Cover Japan 2006

CL: シェフからのお話 Chef's talk
CD, CW: 武藤 雄一 Yuichi Muto
AD, D: 安田 由美子 Yumiko Yasuda
D: 岡崎 智弘 Tomohiro Okazaki
D: 藤岡 香織 Kaori Fujioka
I: 大菅 雅晴 Masaharu Ohsuga
DF, SB: アイルクリエイティブ ayrcreative

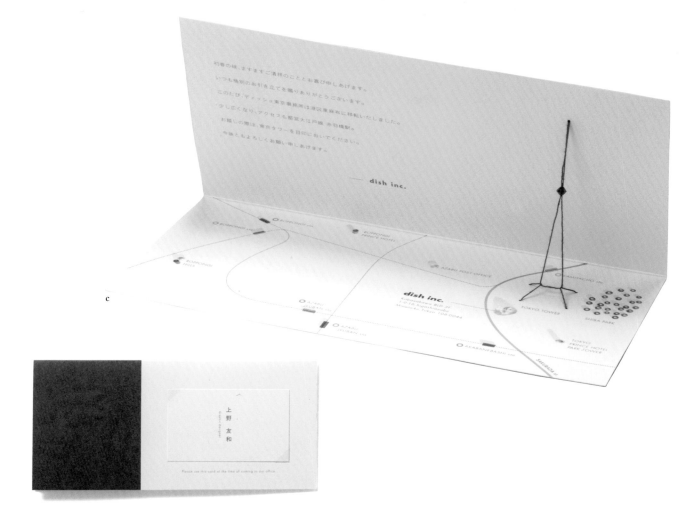

c

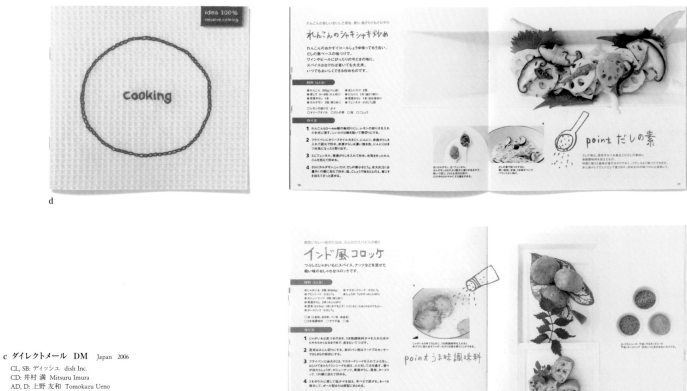

d

c ダイレクトメール **DM** Japan 2006
  CL, SB: ディッシュ dish Inc.
  CD: 井村 満 Mitsuru Imura
  AD, D: 上野 友和 Tomokazu Ueno

d クッキングブック **Cooking Book** Japan 2003
  CL: 味の素 AJINOMOTO Co., Inc.
  AD, D, SB: セルロイド SELLOID Co., Ltd.

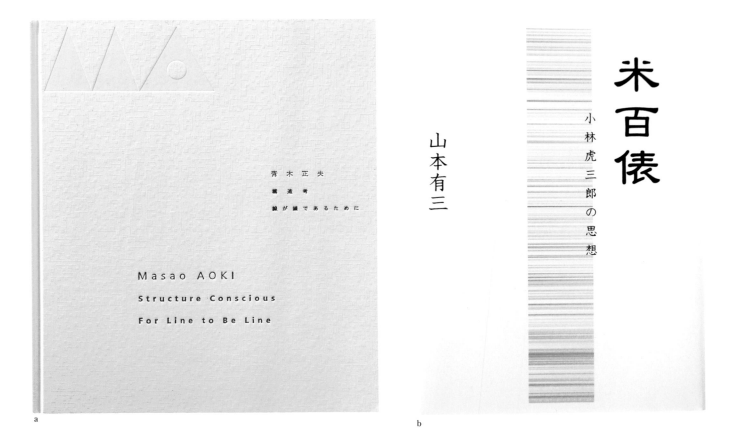

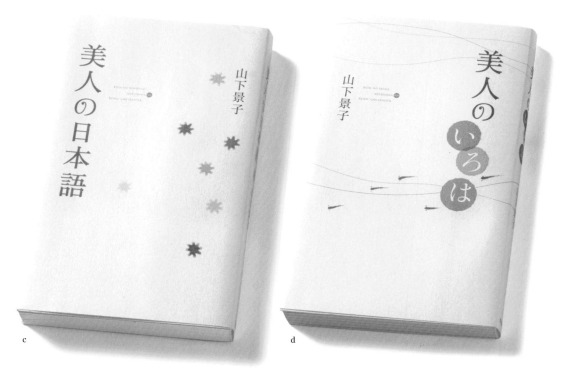

a 装丁 Book Cover Japan 2003
CL, CW: 青木 正夫 Masao Aoki
AD, D, SB: 工藤 強勝 Tsuyokatsu Kudo
D: 伊藤 滋章 Shigeaki Ito
DF: デザイン実験室 Design Laboratory

b 装丁 Book Cover Japan 2003
CL: 長岡市 Nagaoka City
CD: 山本 敦 Atsushi Yamamoto
AD, D: 大川 直人 Naoto Ookawa
Agency: 北越印刷株式会社 HOKUETSU PRINTING Co., Ltd.
DF, SB: ネオス NEOS Co., Ltd.

c, d 装丁 Book Cover Japan 2005 (c), 2006 (d)
CL, SB: 幻冬舎 GENTOSHA Inc.
AD, D: 松岡 史恵 Fumie Matsuoka
I: 吉富 貴子 Takako Yoshitomi

ArjoWiggins PRINT Collection

一枚の存在感。

アルジョウィギンス・プリントコレクション

平和紙業株式会社／アルジョウィギンス・ファインペーパー社

e

iPod Fan Book *Deluxe*

Yasuyuki Wakuni
Mainichi Communications

f

encounter

katsumi omori

g

tsukuyomi   sakiko nomura

h

e カタログ Catalogue　Japan 2004
　CL: アルジョウィギンス　ARJOWIGGINS K.K.
　AD, D: 塚本 明彦　Akihiko Tsukamoto
　CW: 蓑田 雅之　Masayuki Minoda
　DF, SB: 図案倶楽部　Zuan Club

f 装丁 Book Cover　Japan 2005
　CL: 毎日コミュニケーションズ　Mainichi Communications Inc.
　AD: 中島 浩　Hiroshi Nakajima
　DF, SB: ブランク　Plank Co., Ltd.

g, h 装丁 Book Cover　Japan 2005
　CL, SB: マッチアンドカンパニー　match and company
　AD: 町口 覚　Satoshi Machiguchi
　P: 大森克己　Katsumi Omori (g) ／ 野村佐紀子　Sakiko Nomura (h)

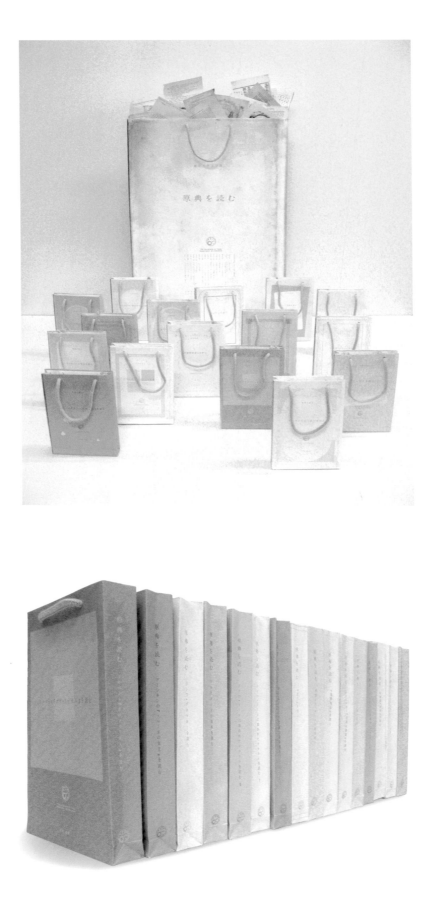

ポスター **Poster** Japan 2004
CL: 東京大学 TOKYO UNIVERSITY
CD: 吉水 雅樹 Masaki Yoshimizu
AD: 森本 千絵 Chie Morimoto
D: 宮脇 亮 RYo Miyawaki / 稲吉 麻衣 Mai Inayoshi
SB: 博報堂クリエイティブヴォックス HAKUHODO CREATIVE VOX Inc.

print & publishing   signage systems
~~ging & promotion   exhibition & display
~~media   interior environment

flight creative

studio 14/15 inkerman street st kilda victoria 3182
lisa nankervis 0408 220 473
telephone (03) 9534 4690 facsimile (03) 9593 6029
mail@flightcreative.com.au www.flightcreative.com.au

a

flying dreams are always the most magnificent

b

takata:
who we are and
where we are going

takata:
who we are and
where we are going

history

大きな判断をするとき、
私たちの先輩たちは
「命に関わるもの」「命を守るもの」に
関わることを選択してきたようです。

織物と釣り糸から始まった「高田工場」が
つくってきたもの:
船舶救命索、パラシュートの緑とベルト、
ホース、シートベルト、人造血管、
エアバッグ、チャイルドシート…

時代の要請や商売上の都合もあったと
思います。しかし、これらはみな人の
命を守り、つなぐものです。
この、人の命に関わるものの方へと
偏重する、度重なるその選択は、
私たちの性質、というか、いっそ「習性」
とでも言える気がしてなりません。

特に、ウェビングの技術を生かした
シートベルトへの着手と
その後の追求は私たちの進む方向を
はっきりと決めました。
このときから、私たちは私たちの
この習性を深めていったのだと思います。

b パンフレット Pamphlet Japan 2005
　CL: タカタ Takata Corporation
　CD, CW: 神谷 幸之助 Kounosuke Kamitani
　AD: 井上 広一 Koichi Inoue (ORYEL)
　P: 岡田 初彦 Hatsuhiko Okada / 鈴木 崇史 Takashi Suzuki (amana)
　CW: John McCreery
　Agency, SB: ワイデン＋ケネディ トウキョウ Wieden+Kennedy Tokyo

a 名刺 Business Card Australia 2003
　CL, AD, D, I, CW, Agency, DF, SB: Flight Creative

NTT Solco ⊙

「 お 客 様 の 声 」 っ て 、 い っ た い 誰 が 聞 い て る の 。

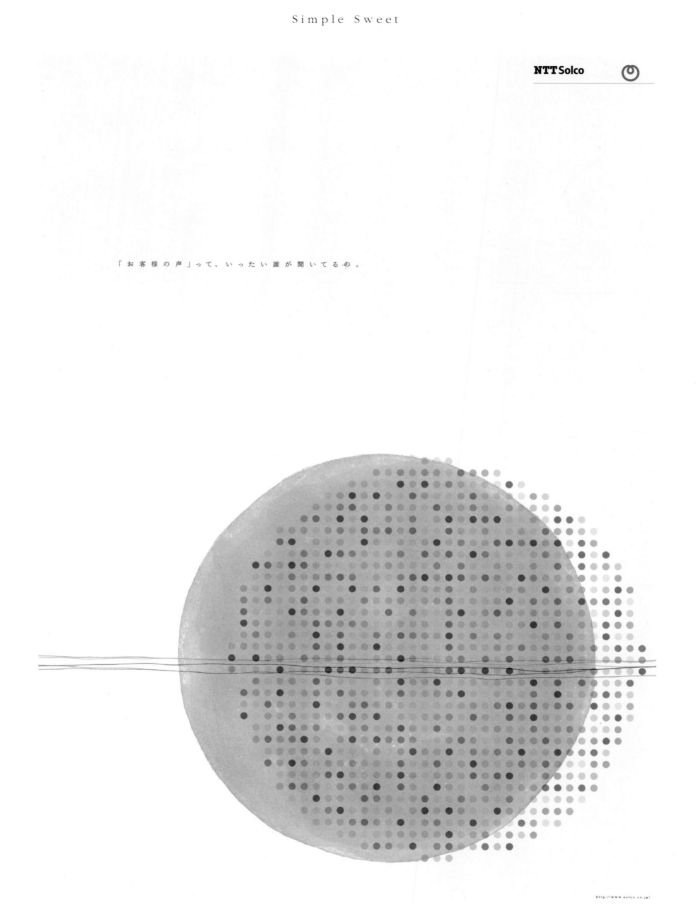

http://www.solco.co.jp/

ポスター Poster Japan 2006
CL: エヌ・ティ・ティ・ソルコ NTT Solco
CD: 高田 禎貴 Yoshitaka Takada
CD, CW: 鵜久森 徹 Toru Ugumori
AD, D, I: 関 宙明 Hiroaki Seki
Agency: NTTアド NTT AD INC.
DF: パイロン PYLON CO., LTD.
SB: ミスター・ユニバース Mr. Universe

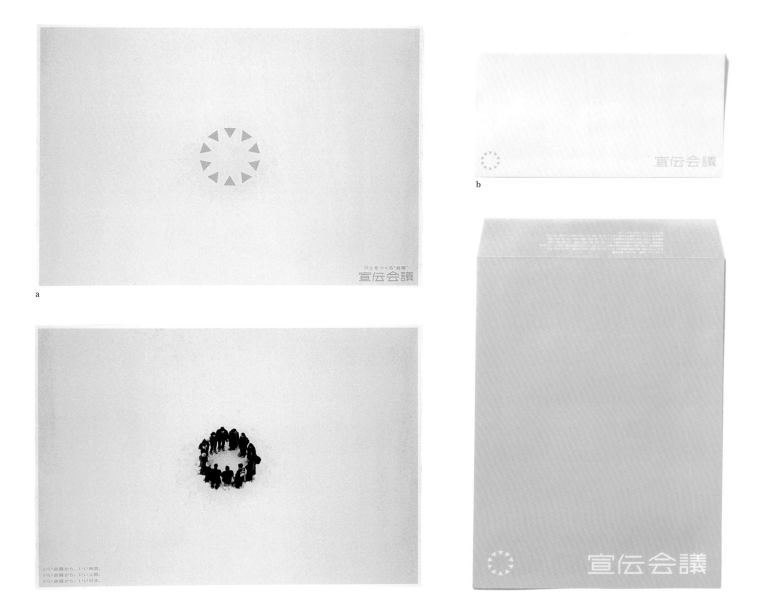

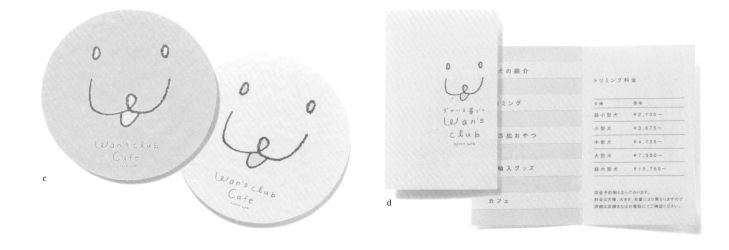

a ポスター　Poster
b 封筒　Envelope　Japan 2004
　CL: 宣伝会議　SENDENKAIGI Co., Ltd.
　AD: 副田 高行　Takayuki Soeda
　D: 中本 陽子　Yoko Nakamoto (a)
　SB: 副田デザイン制作所　SOEDA DESIGN FACTORY

c コースター　Coaster
d ショップカード　Shop Card　Japan 2006
　CL: ワンズクラブ　wan's club
　CD: 山口 不二夫　Fujio Yamaguchi
　AD, D, SB: 宮田 裕美詠　Yumiyo Miyata
　DF: ストライド　STRIDE

a

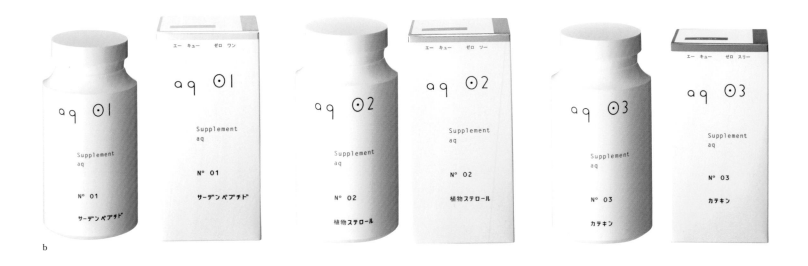

b

a パッケージ　Package　Japan 2007

CL: ウィル・コーポレーション　WELL CORPORATION
CD, DF, SB: トーキョウ・グレート・ヴィジュアル　Tokyo Great Visual Inc.
AD, D, DF: トーキョウ・グレート・ヴィジュアル 大阪　Tokyo Great Visual Inc. Osaka

b パッケージ　Package　Japan 2004

CL: アークレイ　ARKRAY, Inc.
AD, D, SB: グラフ　GRAPH Co., Ltd.
AD, D: 北川 一成　Issay Kitagawa
AD, D: 松本 悟史　Satoshi Matsumoto / 相馬 佑　Yu Soma

パッケージ Package   Japan 2006

CL, SB: エテュセ Et tu sais Co., Ltd.
CD, AD: 平林 奈緒美 Naomi Hirabayashi
D: 斗ヶ沢 哲雄 (ボトルデザイン) Tetsuo Togasawa (Bottle Design)
　　米山 菜津子 (ラベルデザイン) Natsuko Yoneyama (Label Design)

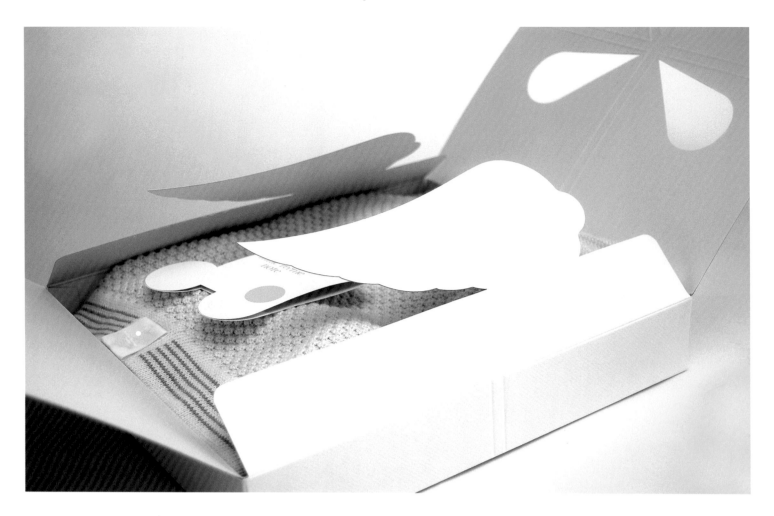

a パッケージ　Package
CD: 千畑 博信　Hironobu Chibata
AD: 岡 記生　Norio Oka
D: 岡 公美　Kumi Oka
DF, SB: デザインユニット リ・ビーンズ　Design Unit RE-Beans

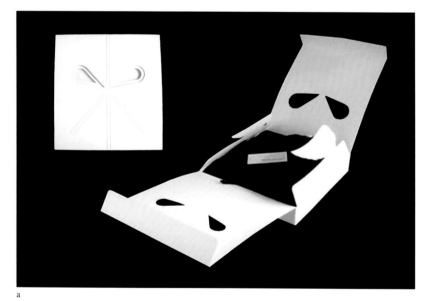

a

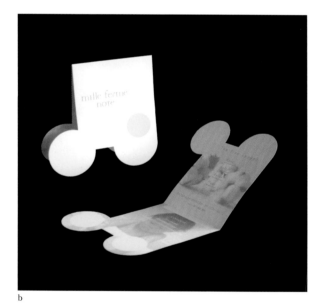

b

a パッケージ　Package
b ショップカード　Shop Card　Japan　2005
CL: CSP Co., Ltd.
CD: 千畑 博信　Hironobu Chibata
AD: 岡 記生　Norio Oka
D: 岡 公美　Kumi Oka
DF, SB: デザインユニット リ・ビーンズ　Design Unit RE-Beans

パッケージ **Package**　China　2006

CL: Cinzia Maini
AD: Joseph Rossi
D, Agency: GraphicFirstAid
Agency, SB: joseph rossi

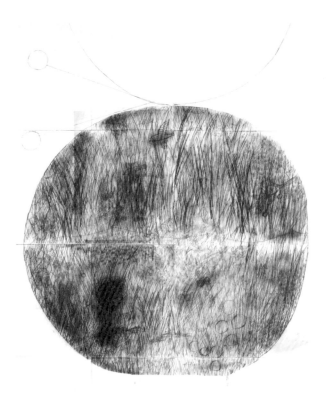

a

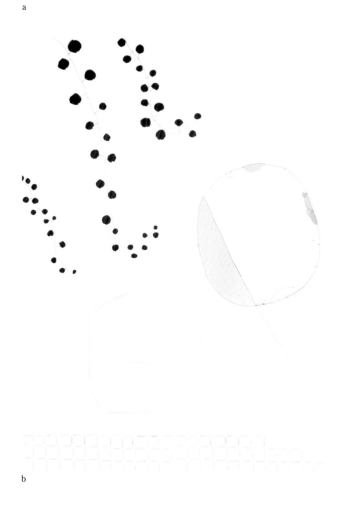

b

a, b ポスター　Poster　Japan　2005 (a), 2006 (b)
CL: JAGDA 富山　JAGDA TOYAMA
AD, D, I, SB: 宮田 裕美詠　Yumiyo Miyata
CW: 川井 昭夫　Akio Kawai (a)
DF: ストライド　STRIDE

a チラシ Flyer
b ステーショナリー Stationery　China　2007

CL: il bello
AD, D: Eric Chan
D: Iris Yu / Manson Chan
I: Lu Lu Ngie (a)
DF, SB: Eric Chan Design Co., Ltd.

パッケージ **Package**   Dubai 2005
CL: Grand Hyatt
AD: Mary Lewis
D: Hideo Akiba / Fiona Verdon-Smith
DF, SB: Lewis Moberly

Simple Colorful

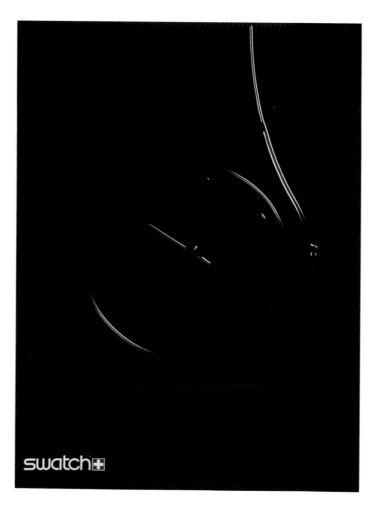

ポスター Poster　Japan　2005
CL: スウォッチ・ジャパン　SWATCH JAPAN Co., Ltd.
CD, AD: 水谷 孝次　Koji Mizutani
D: 紅林 宏和　Hirokazu Kurebayashi
Agency: コスモ コミュニケーションズ　Cosmo Communications
DF, SB: 水谷事務所　Mizutani Studio

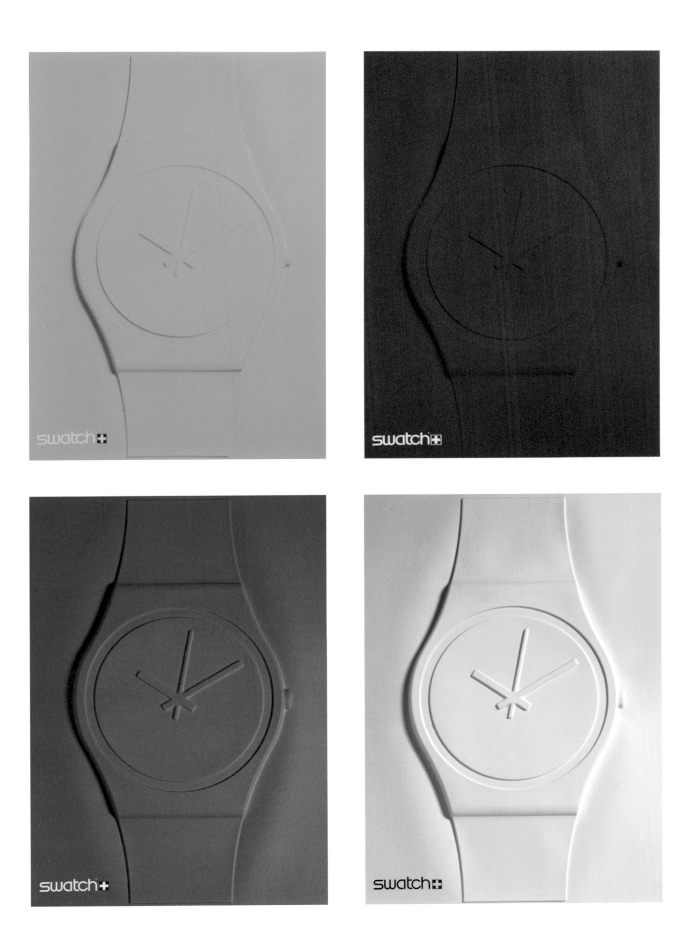

アニュアルレポート　Annual Report　USA　2003

CL: Neoforma Inc.
AD: Bill Cahan
AD, D: Michael Braley
P: Jack McDonald
CW: Kathy Cooper Parker
DF, SB: Cahan & Associates

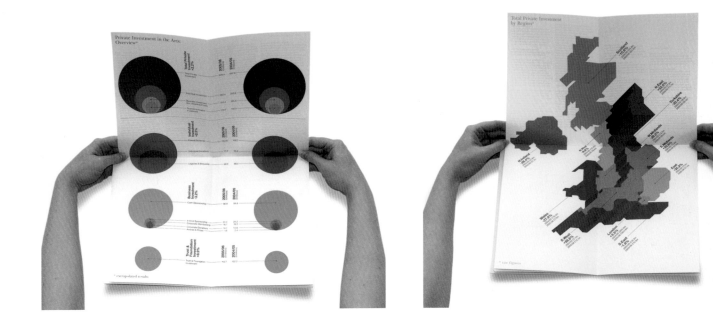

パンフレット **Pamphlet** UK 2006 - 2007

CL: Art & Business
AD: Paul West
AD, D: Paula Benson
D, I: Andy Harvey
DF, SB: Form

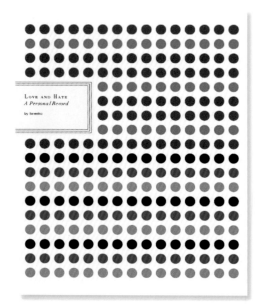

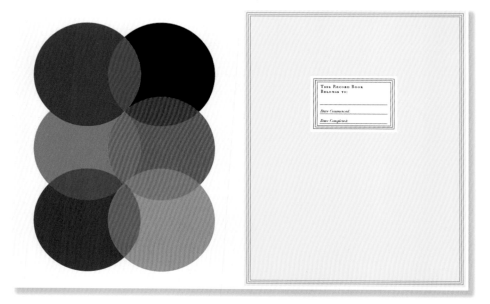

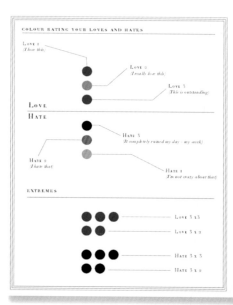

The towns people made were restless with their acrobat being in the middle so they decided to hoist sticky notes of everything they love and everything they hate up to the acrobat which he attached to his athletic outfit. Eventually the entire surface of the acrobats attire was covered with a certain uncertainty. We invented this record book as a handy way of creating your own lists of love and hate without having to go to all the trouble of inventing a town in the middle of no where and erecting some towers and hiring an acrobat and all that.

Everything you love and everything you hate can be summarized here in your record book.

Tweeko

装丁 **Book Cover**   UK   2005
CL: Tweeko
AD, D: Jonathan Howells
DF, SB: Dinnick & Howells

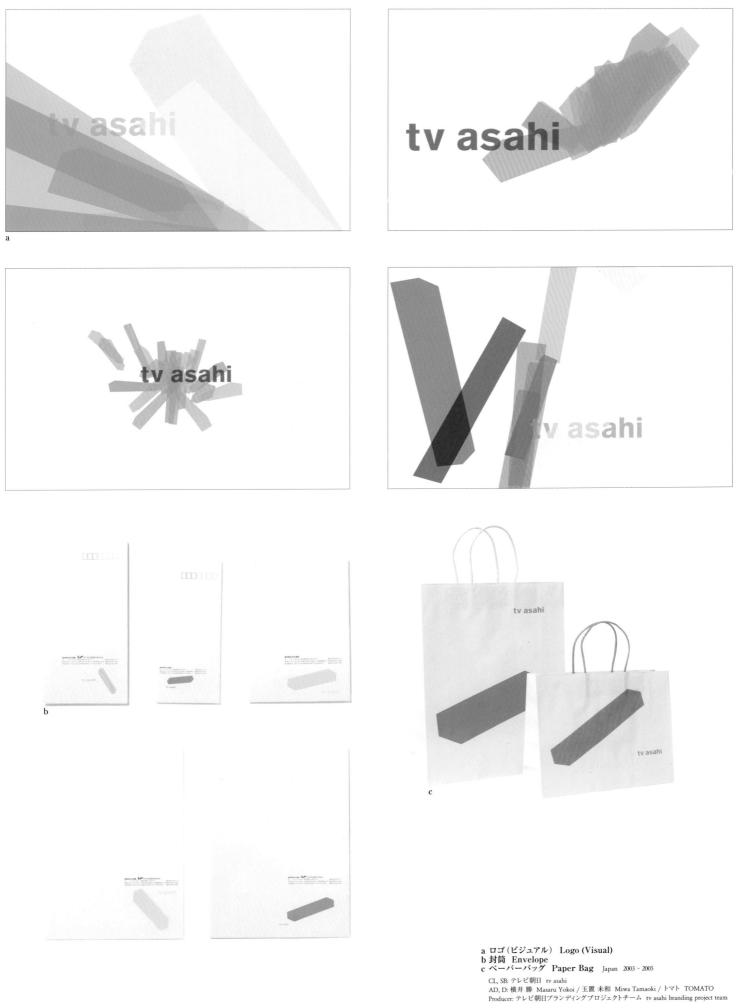

a ロゴ（ビジュアル）　Logo (Visual)
b 封筒　Envelope
c ペーパーバッグ　Paper Bag　Japan　2003 – 2005

CL, SB: テレビ朝日　tv asahi
AD, D: 横井 勝　Masaru Yokoi ／ 玉置 未和　Miwa Tamaoki ／ トマト　TOMATO
Producer: テレビ朝日ブランディングプロジェクトチーム　tv asahi branding project team

アニュアルレポート **Annual Report** Italy 2003

CL: sinv
AD: Joseph Rossi
D, Agency: GraphicFirstAid
Agency, SB: joseph rossi

a

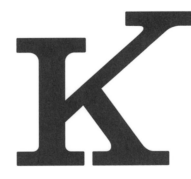

b

a 雑誌広告 Magazine Ad   Japan 2004
CL: インターオフィス Inter Office
CD: 大島 征夫 Yukio Oshima
AD, D: 細谷 巌 Gan Hosoya
D: 竹村 朋子 Tomoko Takemura
P: 宮永 慶太 Keita Miyanaga
CW: 芳谷 兼昌 Kanemasa Yoshitani
SB: ライトパブリシティ Light Publicity Co., Ltd.

b 賞状 Testimonial   Japan 2003
CL: 日本産業デザイン振興会 勝見勝賞事務局
Japan Industrial Design Promotion Organization Katzumie Masaru Award Comittee
AD, D: 細谷 巌 Gan Hosoya
D: 細川 武久 Takeshita Hosokawa
SB: ライトパブリシティ Light Publicity Co., Ltd.

ブローシャー **Brochure** Germany 2002

CL: Esselte Leitz Gmb H Co. KG
AD: Michael Deckelmann
I: Martin Kahrmann
Agency, DF: Campaneros Werbeagentur
SB: Campaneros Werbeagentur Gmb H

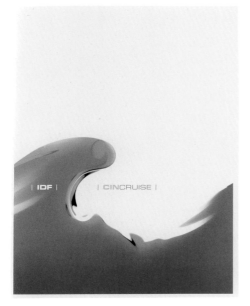

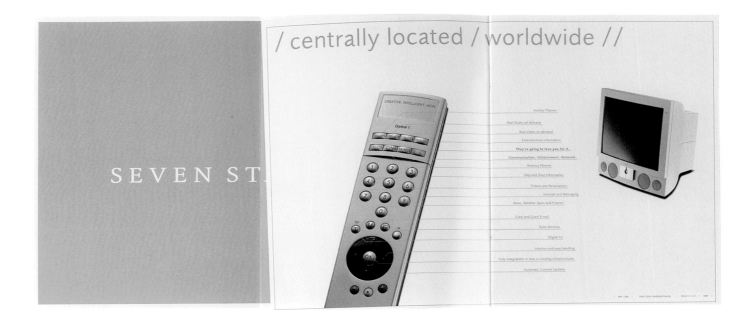

ブローシャー **Brochure** Germany 2002

CL: IDF (Image Design Factory)
AD: Michael Deckelmann
I: Martin Kahrmann
Agency, DF: Campaneros Werbeagentur
SB: Campaneros Werbeagentur Gmb H

a バッケージ　Package

a

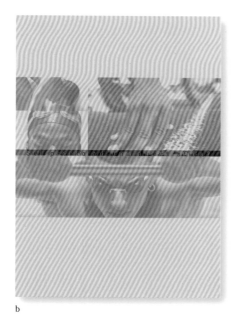

b

a パッケージ　Package
b ブローシャー　Brochure　Italy　2005
　　CL: P&G Prestige Products
　　AD: Mario Rullo / Mario Fois
　　D: Simone Peccédi
　　Agency, DF: Vertigo Design
　　SB: Vertigo Design s.r.l.

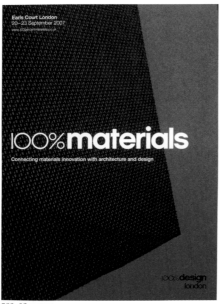

523_02_e.eps

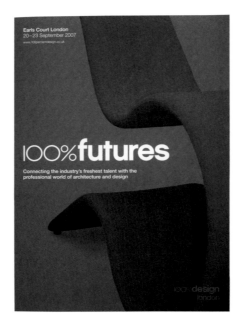

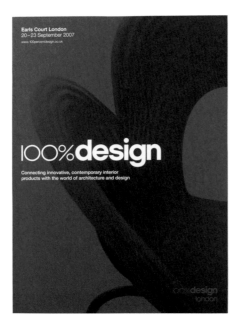

There is no other show that connects the worlds of architecture and design with innovative contemporary interior products, creativity and an exciting mix of new and established talent. The 400 exhibitors in 2006 ranged from international names such as Artek to new textile artist Laura McCafferty. Large and small companies alike choose 100% Design to launch new products and unveil their latest collections. It's also a chance to do business, with many companies taking orders and serious enquiries at the show, and reporting sales throughout the following year as a direct result of exhibiting.

For a show that has built its reputation on innovation and inspiration, 2007 looks set to be an extraordinary year. Alongside the established shows, 100% Futures will be launched, an exciting showcase of the very best new talent looking to step onto the first rung of the design ladder. It means that 100% Design London 2007 will be unmissable for exhibitors and visitors alike.

リーフレット Leaflet UK 2007

CL: 100% Design (Reed Exhibitions)
AD: Angus Hyland
DF, SB: Pentagram

a

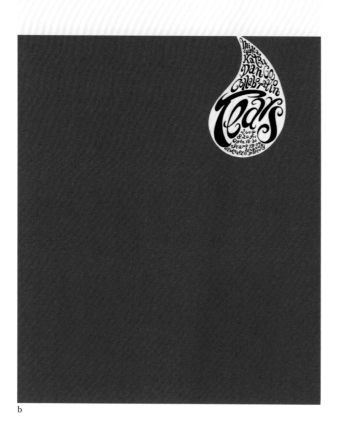

b

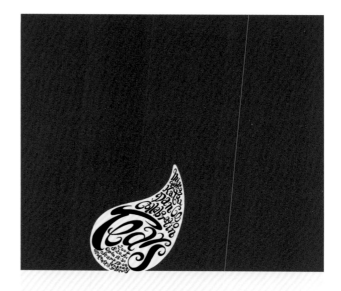

a ポスター Poster　Japan　2006

　CL: フリッツ ハンセン ジャパン Fritz Hansen japan
　AD: 池田 享史 Takafumi Ikeda
　CW: 藤城 敦子 Atsuko Fujishiro
　Agency, DF, SB: デザイン サービス design service Co., Ltd.

b ポスター Poster　Japan　2004

　CL: 加藤みや子ダンススペース MIYAKO KATOH DANCE SPACE
　AD, D, SB: 国定 勝利 Katsutoshi Kunisada

c

d

e

c ノートブック **Notebook** Switzerland 2007

CL: Lift Conference
AD, D, CW: Cristiana Bolli-Freitas
D: Laurent Bolli
I: Mathias Forbach / Gael Vulliens
Agency, DF: Bread-and-Butter.ch
SB: Bread and Butter

d ステーショナリー **Stationery**
e 名刺 **Business Card** Japan 2006

CL: 宮本 昭二 Shoji Miyamoto
AD: 美澤 修 Osamu Misawa
D: 竹内 衛 Mamoru Takeuchi
SB: 美澤修デザイン室 osamu misawa designroom Co., Ltd.

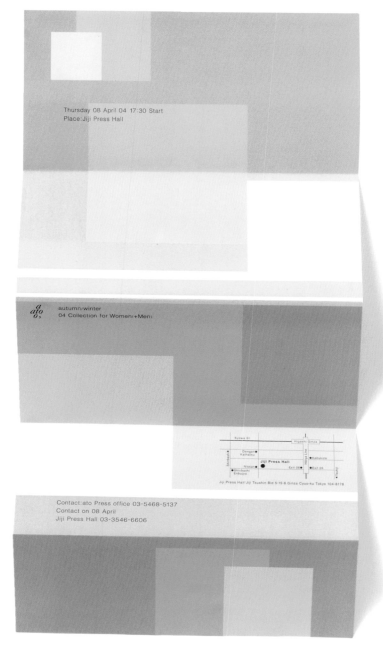

ダイレクトメール　DM　Japan　2004
CL: アトウ　ato
AD, D: 草谷 隆文　Takafumi Kusagaya
D: 金坂 義之　Yoshiyuki Kanesaka
DF, SB: 草谷デザイン　Kusagaya Design Inc.

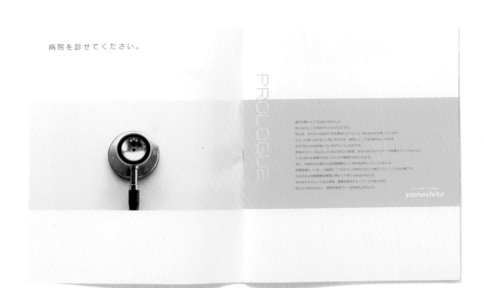

会社案内 Company Brochure Japan 2006
CL: 山下医科機械 YAMASHITA MEDICAL INSTRUMENTS Co., Ltd.
CD, CW: 近藤 成亀 Naruki Kondo
AD: 阿部 純一 Junichi Abe
D: 本山 俊一 Syunichi Motoyama
P: 新出 一真 Kazuma Shinde
Agency: アサツーディ・ケイ九州支社 ASATSU-DK Inc. FUKUOKA OFFICE
DF, SB: キャリーアウト CARRY OUT

a 招待状 **Invitation** Canada 2007

   CL: Marais Miller
   AD, D: Denis Dulude
   DF, SB: Dulude Design

b パンフレット **Pamphlet** Australia 2004 - 2007

   CL: Municipal Association of Victoria
   AD: Tony Ericson / Saskia Ericson
   D, I: Glen McClay
   DF, SB: Hatch Creative

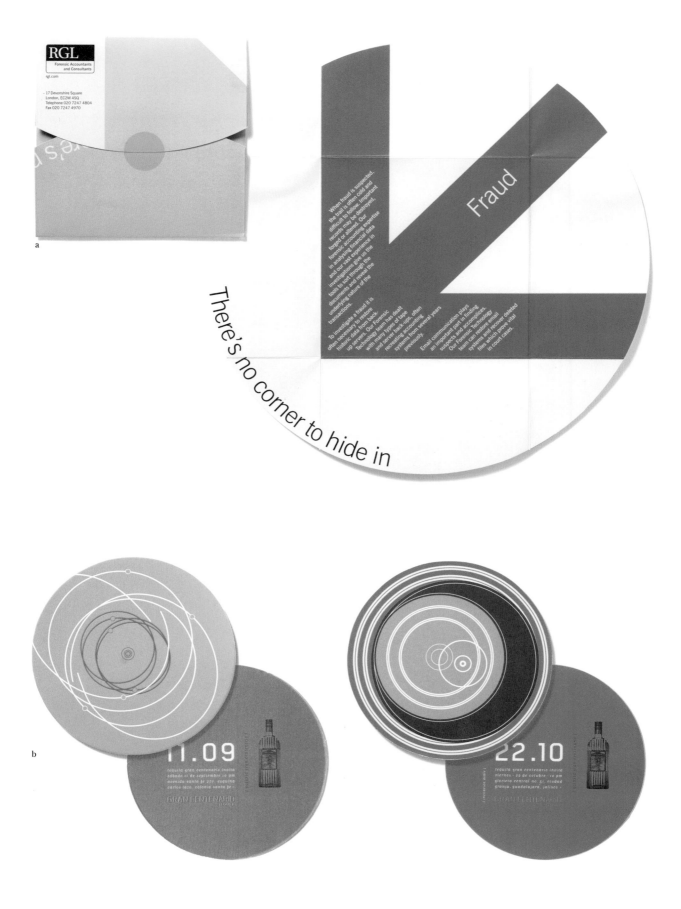

a ダイレクトメール DM　UK 2006
CL: RGL
D: James Alexander
DF: Jade Design
SB: Jade Design Consultants

b 招待状 Invitation　Mexico 2003
CL: Cuervo
CD, D: Vanessa Eckstein
D: Vanesa Enriquez
DF, SB: Bløk Design

a

b

c

d

a ショップバッグ **Shop Bag** Japan 2004
CL: ディノス Dinos Inc.
CD, AD: 水野 学 Manabu Mizuno
D: 上村 昌 Masaru Uemura
DF, SB: グッドデザインカンパニー good design company

b ショップバッグ **Shop Bag**
c ボックス **Box** Japan 2005
CL: クーゲ COUGUE Co., Ltd.
CD, AD: 水谷 孝次 Koji Mizutani
D: 栗谷川 舞 Mai Kuriyagawa
Agency, DF, SB: 水谷事務所 Mizutani Studio

d ショップバッグ **Shop Bag** Italy 2004
CL: Tiscali S.P.A.
D: Justus Oehler / Pentagram Partner
Assistant Designer: Uta Tjaden
SB: Pentagram Design Ltd.

e カタログ **Catalogue** USA 2006
CL: UNIQLO USA / MPC
CD : Kashiwa Sato (Cover Artwork)
AD: Katia Kuethe / Philipp Muessigmann
D: Sidsel Eriksen / Mkrcel Baer
P: Ben Pogue / Alexei Hay Et. Al
I: Bernd Schifferdecker
CW: Matt Smith
Agency: MPC
DF, SB: Studio Von Birken

a

b

b パンフレット　Pamphlet　Portugal　2007
CL: Alquimia da Cor
AD: Antero Ferreira
D: Hugo Morais
D, I: Filipe Sequeira
CW: Jorge Martinho / Alexandra Pinto
DF, SB: Antero Ferreira Design

a 招待状　Invitation　UK　2005
CL: Media Guardian
AD, D: Paul West
D: Claire Warner
SB: Form

c ステーショナリー　Stationery　UK　2007
CL: Granite Color LTD.
AD , D: Paula West / Paula Benson
D: Claire Warner / Nick Hard
D, DF, SB: Form

d DM　USA　2003
CL, CW, SB: Cahan & Associates
AD: Bill Cahan / Bob Dinetz
D: Bob Dinez
CW: David Stolberg

c

d

The Money Pit

The marketing dollars go in and then there's a terrible silence, falling, falling, falling—never to be heard from again. How are you to explain where the money went and what it bought? What about all those big meetings on ROI? Where's the justification? The Money Pit is just one of the levels of marketing hell you are all too familiar with. And from which you have suffered too long.

www.getoutofhell.com

The Endowment for the Arts

That's how some strategic design agencies view you. You are the Marketing Medici here to finance their vision. It's art not for sales sake or brand building sake but rather for the sake of a couple of people out to win another Art Directors Club award. On your dime. The Endowment for the Arts is just one of the levels of marketing hell you are all too familiar with. And from which you have suffered too long.

www.getoutofhell.com

Clawing Your Way to the Middle

Welcome to the middle ground—the land of average and ho-hum. It's where you end up when your marketing partner gives good meetings and brilliantly manages process—but forgets (or isn't capable of) unearthing an inspired perspective. Clawing Your Way to the Middle is just one of the levels of marketing hell you are all too familiar with. And from which you have suffered too long.

www.getoutofhell.com

Doing Nothing

In challenging times, the inclination is to hit pause, rethink, play it safe. It's only human to do so. But great rewards await those with the courage to act in a way that is unexpected and unpopular. We're inspired by clients who want to make a difference for their products, brands, and companies. We invite you to see where that passion has taken us in our work for the companies we've partnered with. Clients with whom you may have much in common.

www.getoutofhell.com

ダイレクトメール　DM　Japan　2007

CL: 八木通商　Yagi Tsusho Ltd.
　　スープリームス インコーポレーテッド　SUPREMES INCORPORATED
CD: Jet State Inc.
AD: 久住 欣也　Yoshinari Hisazumi (HD LAB Inc.)
D: 坂口 智彦　Tomohiko Sakaguchi (HD LAB Inc.)
DF, SB: HD LAB Inc.

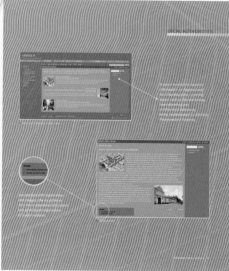

a ポスター Poster
パンフレット Pamphlet UK 2006

CL: Media Trust
AD: Paul West
AD, D: Paula Benson
D: Andy Harvey
DF, SB: Form

b 会社案内 Company Brochure Italy 2006

CL: Agenzia del Demanio
AD: Mario Fois / Mario Rullo
D: Massimo Scacco
Agency, DF: Vertigo Design
SB: Vertigo Design s.r.l.

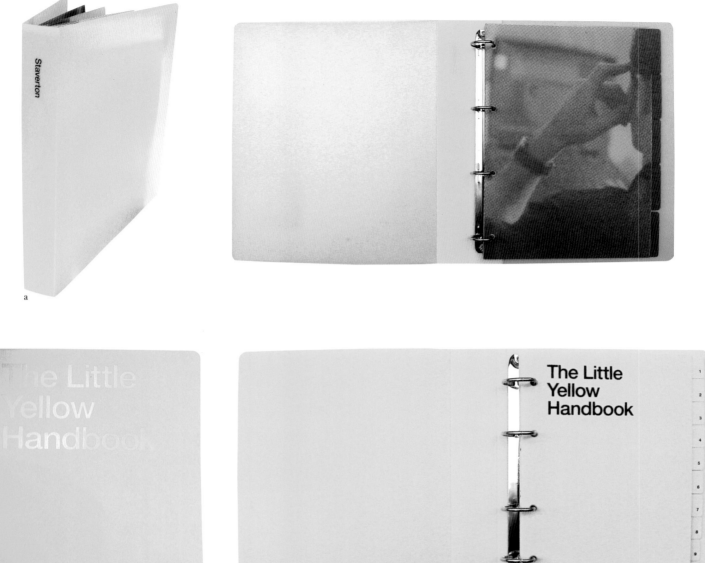

a

b

a ハンドブック Hand Book
b ペーパーバッグ Paper Bag　UK　2006

CL: Staverton LTD
AD, D: Paul West / Paula Benson
DF, SB: Form

a ステーショナリー Stationery USA 2006
CL: The Sorrell Company
D, I, DF, SB: Lizette Gecel
I: Ultimate Symbol

b 名刺 Business Card China 2005
CL: Vgood Co., Ltd.
AD, D: Eric Chan
D: Iris Yu / Manson Chan
I: Lu Lu Ngie
DF, SB: Eric Chan Design Co., Ltd.

a

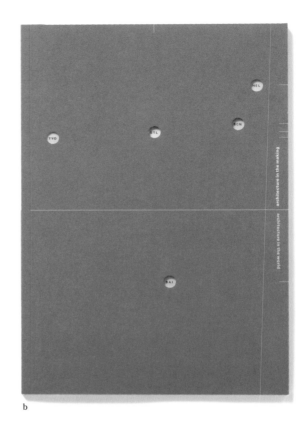

b

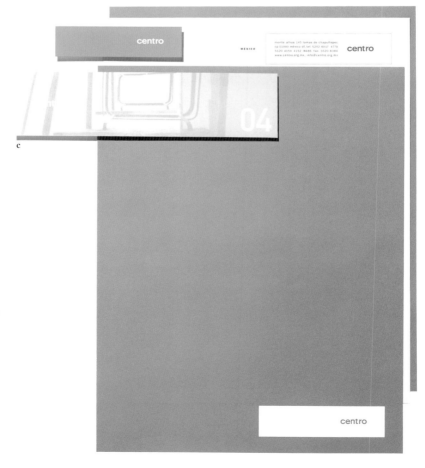

c

a, b カタログ Catalogue USA 2004 (a), 2007 (b)

CL: Washington Univerisity in St. Louis Graduate School of Architecture + Urban Design
AD, D: Jilly Simons
Design Assistant: Regan Blough
P: Various
I: Various
CW: Peter Mackeith
DF, SB: Concrete [The Office of Jilly Simons]
Printer: Active Graphics

c ステーショナリー Stationery Mexico 2003

CL: Centro
CD, D: Vanessa Eckstein
D: Mariana Contegni
P: Colin Faulkner
DF, SB: Bløk Design

minä perhonen 1　textile

ミナ ペルホネン の 織り

文化出版局

minä perhonen 3　print

ミナ ペルホネン の プリント

文化出版局

minä perhonen 2　embroidery

ミナ ペルホネン の 刺繍

文化出版局

装丁　Book Cover　Japan　2005
CL: 文化出版局　Bunka Publishing Bureau
AD: 有山 達也　Tatsuya Ariyama
D: 中島 寛子　Hiroko Nakajima
P: 森本 美絵　Mie Morimoto
SB: アリヤマデザインストア　ariyama design store

a

b

c

d

a, b ポスター Poster   Japan   2006 (a), 2007 (b)

    CL: アミュプラザ長崎 AMU PLAZA NAGASAKI
    CD: 高野 隆一 Ryuichi Takano
    AD: 梶原 道生 Michio Kajiwara
    D: 中島 めぐみ Megumi Nakashima
    I: 天羽間 ソラノ Sorano Amahama
    CW: 安恒 つかさ Tsukasa Yasutsune (a) / 古賀 康子 Yasuko Koga (b)
    Agency: ジェイアール九州エージェンシー JR KYUSHU AGENCY Co., Ltd.
    DF, SB: カジグラ KAJIGRA

c ショップバッグ Shop Bag
d パッケージ Package   UK 2005

    CL: Girls Gorgeous Girls / The Girl Company
    AD: Mary Lewis
    D: Poppy Steadman
    DF: LM
    SB: Lewis Moberly

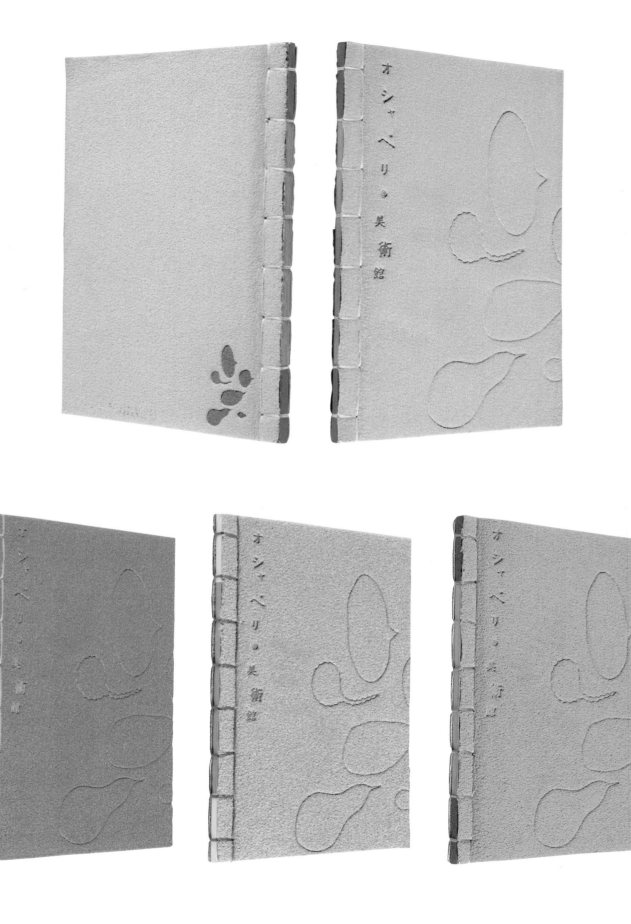

パンフレット **Pamphlet**   Japan   2002
CL: 丸亀市猪熊弦一郎現代美術館
　　Marugame Genichiro-Inokuma Museum of Contemporary Art
AD: 永井 裕明 Hiroaki Nagai
D: 岩田 勇紀 Yuki Iwata
P: 瀧本 幹也 Mikiya Takimoto
Artist: 立花 文穂 Fumio Tachibana
DF, SB: エヌ・ジー N.G. Inc.

カタログ Catalogue   Italy 2003
CL: FLASH & PARTNERS
AD: Joseph Rossi
D, Agency: GraphicFirstAid
P: Sebastiano Pavia
Agency, SB: joseph rossi

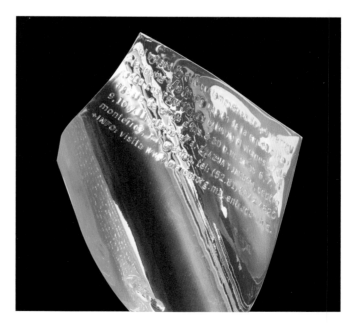

a メニューカバー Menu Cover Japan 2006

CL: デルレイ DEL REY
AD: 池田 享史 Takafumi Ikeda
D: 菅 渉宇 Sho Suga
Agency: PCM竹尾 PCM Takeo. Co., Ltd.
DF, SB: デザインサービス design service Co., Ltd.

b 招待状 Invitation Mexico 2005

CL: Museo Marco
CD, D: Vanessa Eckstein
D: Vanesa Enriquez
DF, SB: Bløk Design

パッケージ **Package** Canada 2007

CL: Aspenware
CD, D: Vanessa Eckstein
AD: Marc Stoiber (Change)
D: Patricia Kleebers
Agency: Change (Canada)
DF, SB: Bløk Design

パッケージ **Package**　Japan 2002
CL: バーンホーフ　BANHOF
CD: 川良 紀彦　Toshihiko Kawara / 入江 信宏　Nobuhiro Irie
AD: シマダ タモツ　Tamotsu Shimada
AD, D: 増永 明子　Akiko Masunaga
P: 平塚 正男　Masao Hiratsuka
SB: シマダデザイン　Shimada Design Inc.

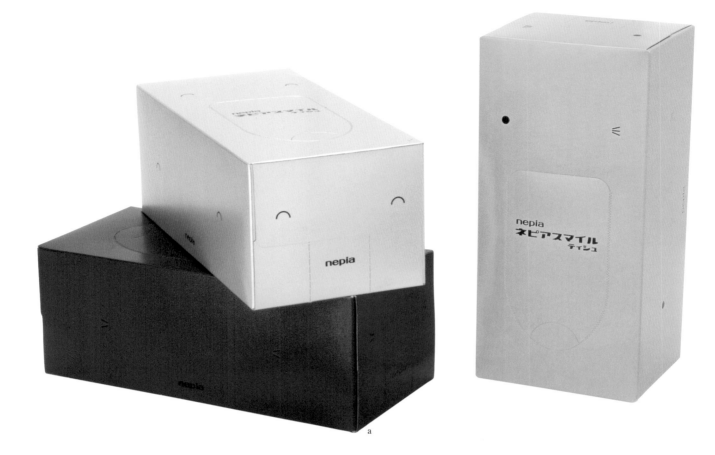

a, b, d パッケージ **Package** Japan 2003 (b, d), 2007 (a)
　　CL: 王子ネピア　Oji nepia Co., Ltd.
　　CD, AD: 田代 嘉宏　Yoshihiro Tashiro
　　D: 中山 祐香　Yuka Nakayama
　　DF, SB: ゴースト　GOEST, Inc.

c パッケージ **Package** Japan 2005
　　CL: アスクル　ASKUL Corporation
　　AD: 田代 嘉宏　Yoshihiro Tashiro
　　D: 中山 祐香　Yuka Nakayama
　　DF, SB: ゴースト　GOEST, Inc.

c

d

a

b

a カップ　Cup
b ショップバッグ　Shop Bag　UK　2002

CL: NIN COM SOUP
AD: Ben Stott / Alan Dye / Nick Finney
D, CW: Alan Dye
SB: NB Studio

a

b

a パッケージ Package　Japan　2007

　CL, SB: キリンビール　Kirin Brewery Co., Ltd.
　CD, AD: 橋本 善司　Zenji Hashimoto
　D: 平井 緑　Midori Hirai / 青木 麻衣子　Maiko Aoki
　DF: クラウドエイト　CLOUD 8 Inc.

b パッケージ Package　Japan　2007

　CL, SB: キリンビール　Kirin Brewery Co., Ltd.
　AD: 髙橋 稔　Minoru Takahashi

c パッケージ Package　USA　2005

　CL: Benjamin Moore
　AD: Bill Thorburn
　D: Ben Levitz / David Schwen
　P: Mark Laita
　DF, SB: Carmichael Lynch Thorburn

c

a パッケージ **Package** Japan 2004

CL, SB: 資生堂 SHISEIDO CO., LTD.
CD, AD: 平戸 絵里子 Eriko Hirato
D: 渡辺 真佐子 Masako Watanabe
P: 金澤 正人 Masato Kanazawa

b パッケージ **Package** Australia 2005

CL, CW: David Jones
AD: Anntte Harcus
D: Marianne Walter
P: Brendan Read
DF, SB: Harcus Design

パッケージ Package 2005
CL, SB: リサージ LISSAGE Ltd.
DF: カラーインク COLOR Inc.

a

b

a パッケージ Package　Japan 2004
　CL, SB: 資生堂 SHISEIDO CO., LTD.
　CD: 工藤 青石 Aoshi Kudo
　AD: 高橋 新三 Shinzo Takahashi
　D: 村田 一平 Ippei Murata / 本田 かほり Kahori Honda

b パッケージ Package　Japan 2004
　CL, SB: 資生堂 SHISEIDO CO., LTD.
　CD, AD: 工藤 青石 Aoshi Kudo
　D: 村田 一平 Ippei Murata / 高橋 新三 Shinzo Takahashi

パッケージ **Package** USA 2003
CL, DF: コル デザイン　Köl Design Co., Ltd.
CD: Sally and Andrew Brunger
SB: シュウエイトレーディング　Shuei Trading Co., Ltd.

a, b, c, d パッケージ　Package　　Japan　2003 (a), 2004 (b, c), 2007 (d)
CL, SB: ローレル　LAUREL CO., LTD.
D: 加藤 めぐみ　Megumi Kato

Simple Modern

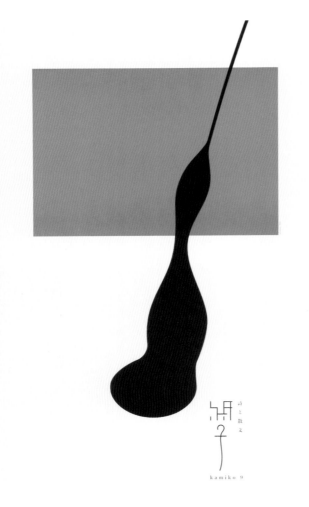

ポスター Poster Japan 2005
CL: 文屋 Bunya
AD, D: 大野 好之 Yoshiyuki Ohno
CW: 荻原 健次郎 Kenjiro Hagiwara
DF, SB: グッドマン goodman inc.

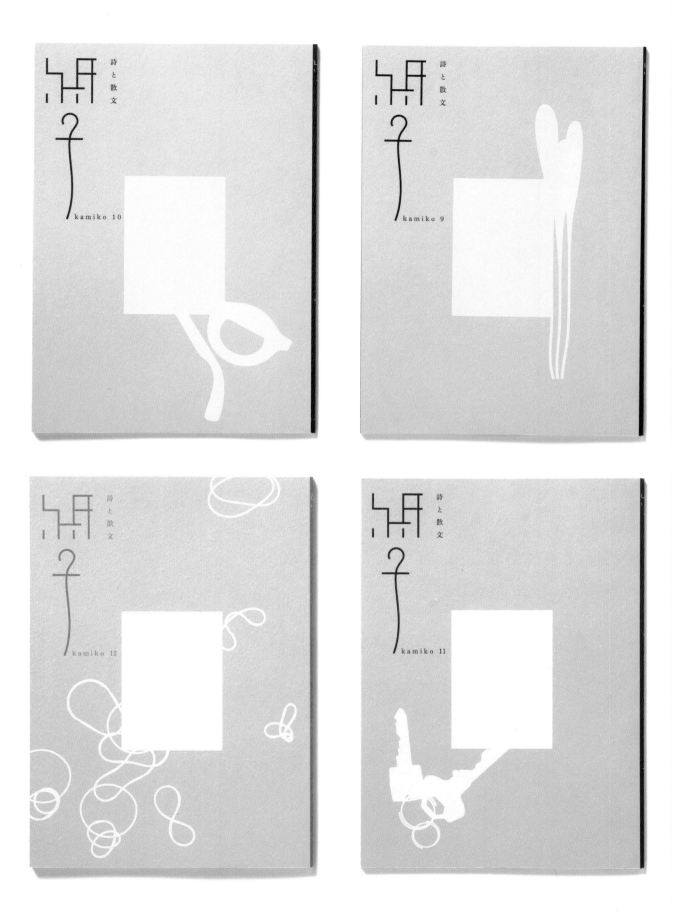

装丁 **Book Cover** Japan 2005
CL: 文屋 Bunya
AD, D: 大野 好之 Yoshiyuki Ohno
CW: 荻原 健次郎 Kenjiro Hagiwara
DF, SB: グッドマン goodman inc.

ポスター Poster   Japan 2005
CL: DAZED & CONFUSED JAPAN
AD, D: 山田 英二 Eiji Yamada
DF, SB: ウルトラグラフィックス ULTRA Graphics

ポスター　Poster　Japan　2004

CL: 8 1/2 Eight & Half
AD, D: 山田 英二 Eiji Yamada
P: 瀧本 幹也 Mikiya Takimoto
DF, SB: ウルトラグラフィックス ULTRA Graphics

a

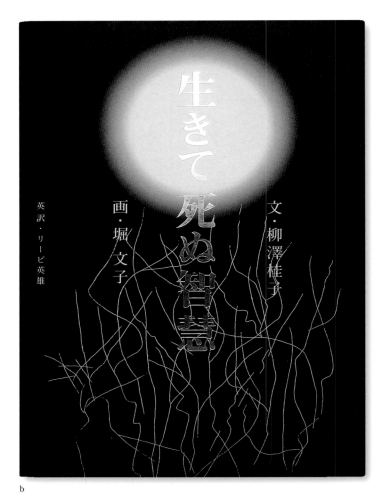

b

a, b 装丁 Book Cover   Japan 2004

CL: 小学館 Syogakukan
AD, D, SB: 高橋 善丸 Yoshimaru Takahashi
DF: 広告丸 KOKOKUMARU. Co., Ltd.

c, d ポスター Poster   Japan 2006

CL, DF, SB: TOKIデザイン室 TOKI DESIGN STUDIO
AD, D: 坪内 祝義 Tokiyoshi Tsubouchi

e, f ポスター Poster   Japan 2006 (e), 2007 (f)

CL: 東京コンサーツ Tokyo Concerts, Inc.
AD, D: 坪内 祝義 Tokiyoshi Tsubouchi
DF, SB: TOKIデザイン室 TOKI DESIGN STUDIO

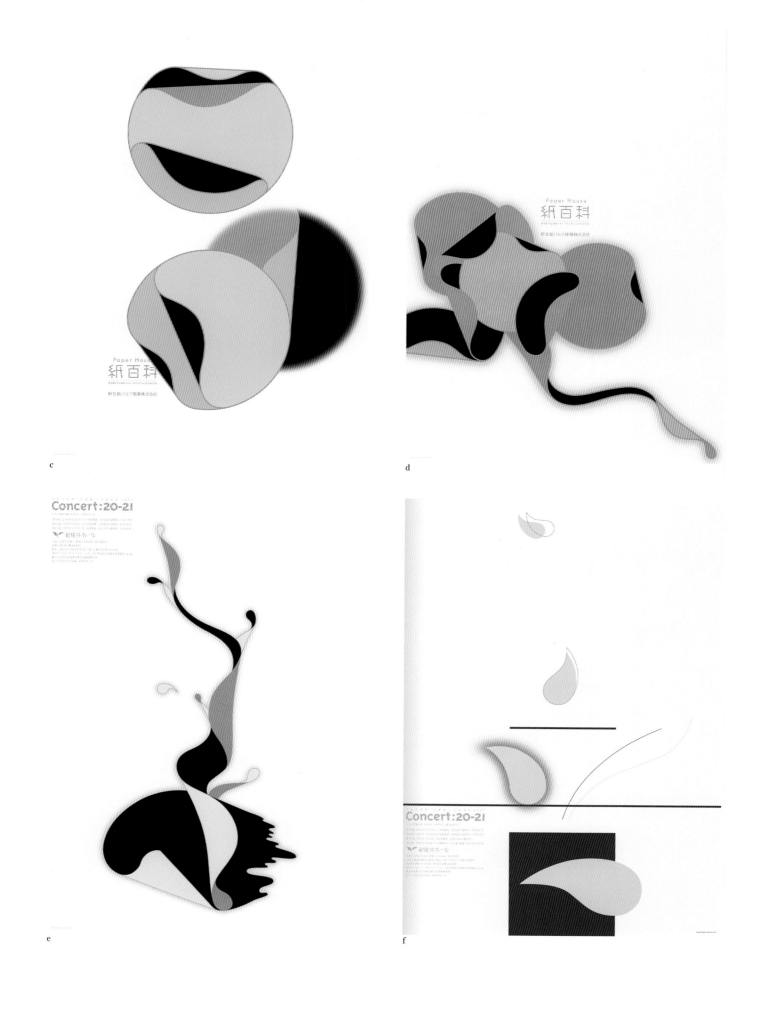

c

d

e

f

パッケージ **Package** Japan 2006
CL: 虎屋 TORAYA CONFECTIONERY Co., Ltd.
CD, AD: 葛西 薫 Kaoru Kasai
D: 櫻井 亮太郎 Ryotaro Sakurai
DF, SB: サン・アド SUN-AD CO., LTD.

a

b

c

d

a パッケージ Package Japan 2007

CL, SB: 丸八製茶場 maruhachi seichajyo
D: スズキ タクミ Takumi Suzuki
Typographer: 井上 珀雲 Hakuun Inoue

b パッケージ Package Japan 2003

CL: 千寿酒造 senju shuzou
AD: 藤田 寿浩 Toshihiro Fujita
D: 川合 正晃 Masaaki Kawai
DF, SB: ブルックスタジオ brook studio Co., Ltd.

c パッケージ Package Japan 2004

CL: 桝一市村酒造場 Masuichi Ichimura Sake Brewery
CD, AD, D: 梅原 真 Makoto Umebara
DF, SB: 梅原デザイン事務所 Umebara Design Office

d パッケージ Package Japan 2005

CL: 富久錦 Fukunishiki Co., Ltd.
AD, D, SB: グラフ GRAPH CO., LTD.
AD, D: 北川 一成 Issay Kitagawa
井上 学 Manabu Inoue

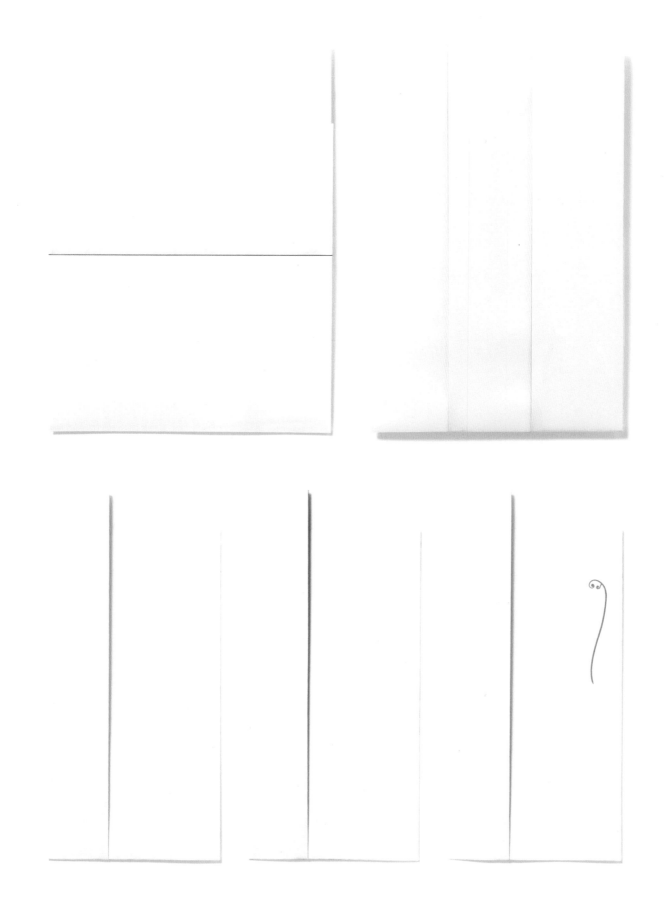

のし袋 **Noshi-bukuro** Japan 2006
CL: 裏具 uragu
AD, D: 大野 好之 Yoshiyuki Ohno
DF, SB: グッドマン goodman inc.

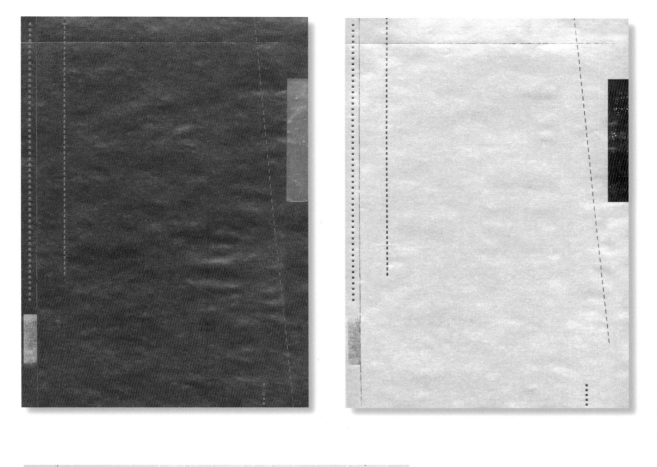

ステーショナリー Stationery Japan 2006
CL: アントワーヌ・ブリュメル ANTOINE BRUMEL
CD: Joan McCulloch
AD, D: 山本 ヒロキ Hiroki Yamamoto
SB: マーヴィン MARVIN Co., Ltd.

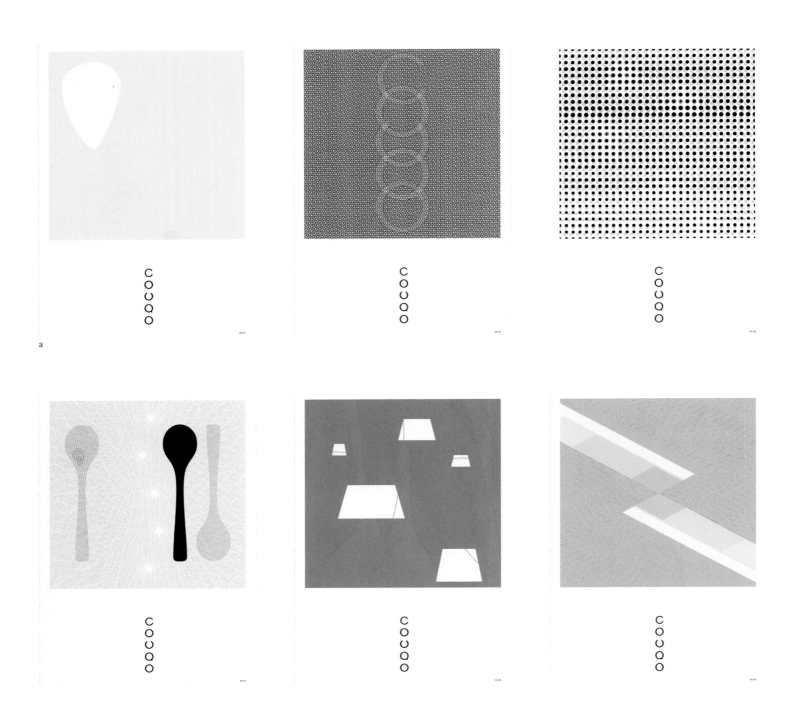

a ポスター　Poster
b ショップカード　Shop Card
c マッチ　Match　Japan　2005

CL: クコ　COUQO
CD: Joan McCulloch
AD, D: 山本 ヒロキ　Hiroki Yamamoto
D: 村上 香　Kaori Murakami / 佐藤 奈穂子　Naoko Sato
SB: マーヴィン　MARVIN Co., Ltd.

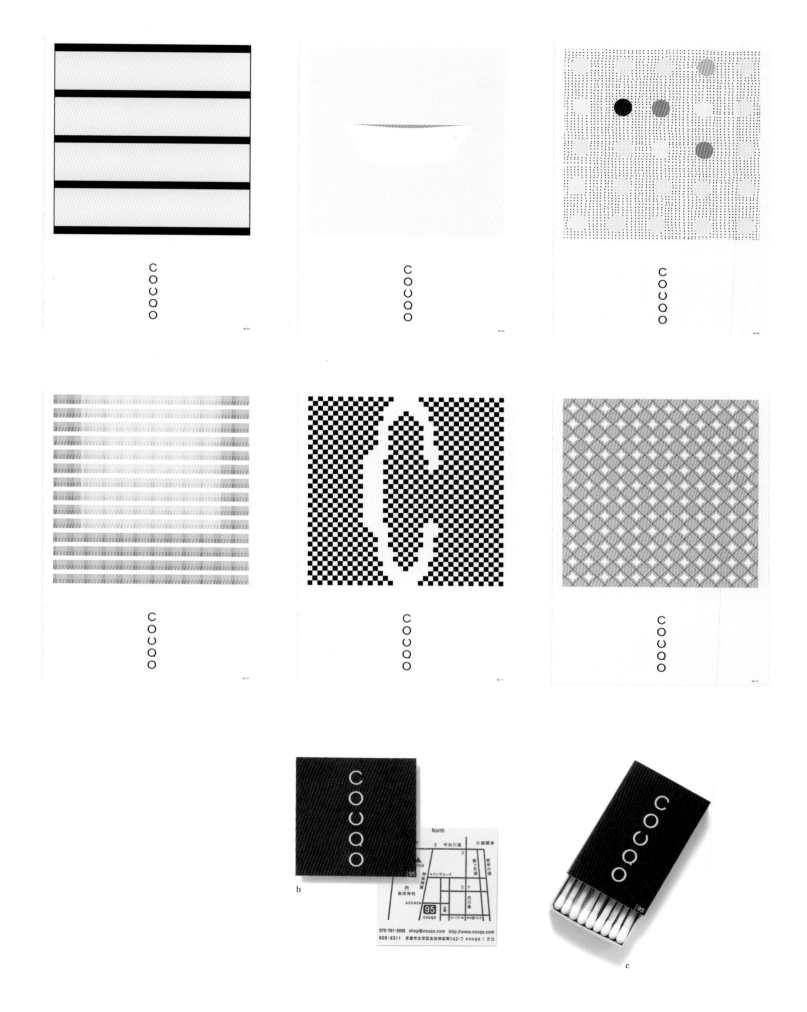

a

b

a 装丁 Book Cover Japan 2002
   CL: 日本文教出版 Nihon Bunkyou Shuppan Co., Ltd.
   CD, AD: 松下 計 Kei Matsushita
   SB: 松下計デザイン室 KEI Matsushita Design Room Inc.

b パンフレット Pamphlet Japan 2004
   CL: 日本青少年文化センター Japan Culture Center for Youths and Children
   AD, D: 大澤 和歌子 Wakako Ohsawa / チャネルジー Channel Z
   CW: 陳 慧 Hui Chen
   DF, SB: アドレッサンス浪漫堂 ADOLESCENCE ROMANDO Co., Ltd.

a

b

a ポスター Poster　Japan　2004
　CL: 大倉三幸　OKURA SANKO CO., LTD.
　AD, D: 坪内 祝義　Tokiyoshi Tsubouchi
　DF, SB: TOKIデザイン室　TOKI DESIGN STUDIO

b ダイレクトメール DM　Japan　2005
　CL, Agency: サヴィー　THAVI Co., Ltd.
　CD, AD: 春高 壽人　Hisato Harutaka
　D: 門司 大典　Daisuke Monji
　CW: 権藤 邦彦　Kunihiko Gondo
　DF, SB: 春高デザイン　HARUTAKA DESIGN

ステーショナリー　Stationery　UK　2006

CL: Wild Circle
AD: Paul West
AD, D: Paula Benson
D: Tom Hutchings
D, DF, SB: Form

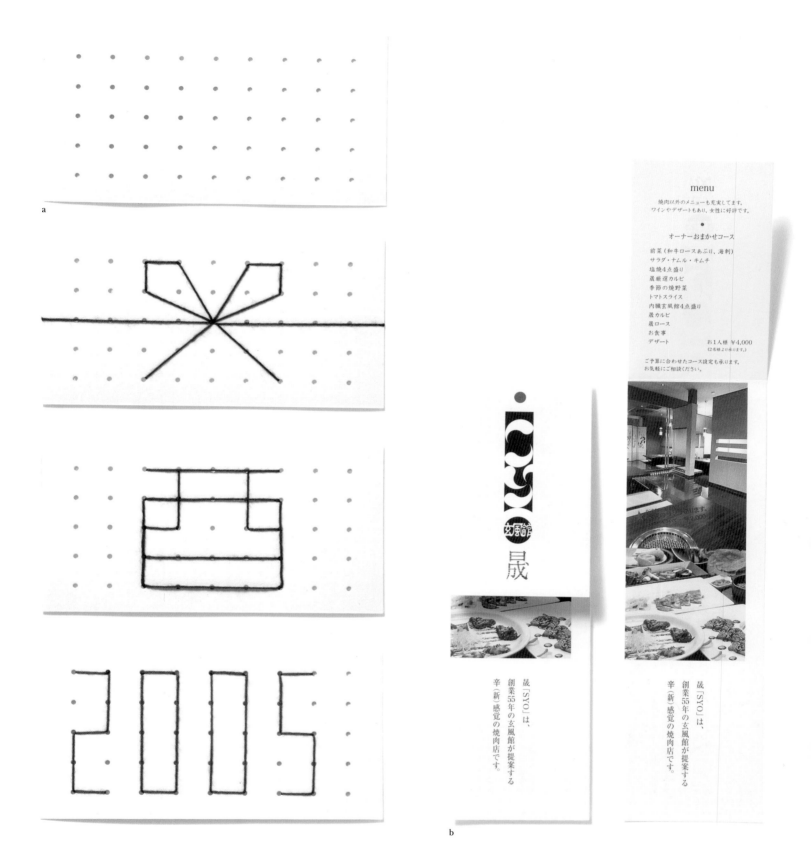

a 年賀状 New Year Greeting Card 2005   Japan 2004
CL: 『デザインの現場』編集部
　　Edition Department of "Designers' Workshop"
AD, D: 高橋 正実 Masami Takahashi
DF, SB: マサミデザイン MASAMI DESIGN

b ショップカード Shop Card   Japan 2005 (a)
CL: 玄風館・晟 GENPUKAN SYO
CD: 原田 有希 Yuki Harada (Shin hye-yong)
DF, SB: クルン curum

a

b

a 装丁 **Book Cover** Japan 2003
CL: 新書館 SHINSHOKAN Publishing Co., Ltd.
CD, I: 楠本 まき Maki Kusumoto
AD, D, SB: 秋田 和徳 Kazvnori Akita

b 賞状 **Testimonial** Japan 2003
CL: 桑沢デザイン研究所 同窓会 Kuwasawa Design School Alumni Association
AD, D, SB: 工藤 強勝 Tsuyokatsu Kudo
D: 伊藤 滋章 Shigeaki Ito
DF: デザイン実験室 Design Laboratory

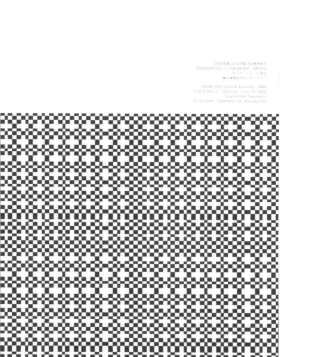

a

b

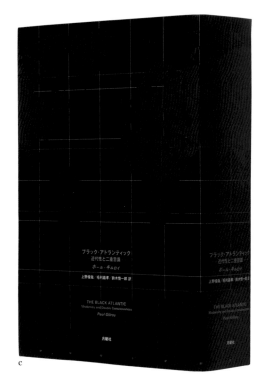

c

a カタログ Catalogue   Japan 2006
CL: 日本グラフィックデザイナー協会
　　Japan Graphic Designers Association Inc.
CD, AD: 松下 計 Kei Matsushita
D: 渡辺 京子 Kyoko Watanabe
SB: 松下計デザイン室 KEI Matsushita Design Room Inc.

b 装丁 Book Cover   USA 2004
CL: Saks 5th Svenue
AD: Gary Tooth
P: Various
CW: Mary Dinaberg
DF, SB: Empire Design Studio

c 装丁 Book Cover   Japan 2006
CL: 月曜社 Getsuyosha Ltd.
CD: 神林 豊 Yutaka Kanbayashi
AD: 中島 浩 Hiroshi Nakajima
DF, SB: ブランク Plank Co., Ltd.

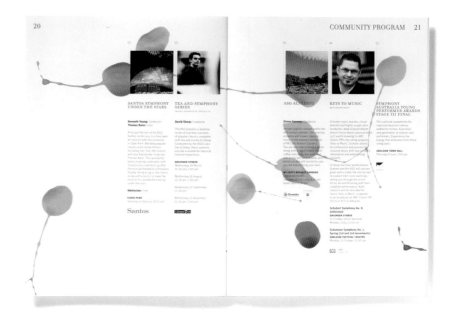

ブローシャー **Brochure** Australia 2005

CL, CW: Adelaide Symphony Orchestra
AD, D: Anthony Deleo
D: Scott Carslake
P: Toby Richardson
I: South Australia School of Arts, 2nd Year Students
I, DF, SB: Voice

a

b

a パンフレット **Pamphlet** UK 2002

  CL: Crafts Council
  AD: Ben Stott / Alan Dye / Nick Finney
  D, CW: Nick Vincent
  P: Thomas Hayward
  SB: NB Studio

b パンフレット **Pamphlet** Switzerland 2007

  CL: Lift Conference
  AD, D, CW: Cristiana Bolli-Freitas
  D: Laurent Bolli
  I: Mathias Forbach / Gael Vulliens
  Agency, DF: Bread-and-Butter.ch
  SB: Bread and Butter

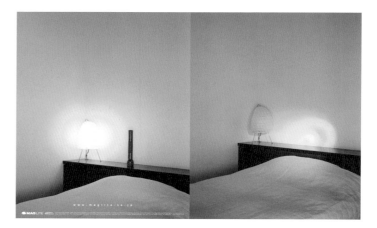

雑誌広告 **Magazine Ad**　Japan　2003
CL: 三井物産　Mitsui & Co., Ltd.
CD, AD: 川口 清勝　Seijo Kawaguchi
D: 不破 稔　Minoru Fuwa
P: 藤井 保　Tamotsu Fujii
DF: BRIDGE
Agency Producer: 佐藤 瑠奈子　Runako Sato (TUGBOAT)
Creative Agency, SB: TUGBOAT

a

b

a リーフレット Leaflet Italy 2005

CL: OmniDecor
AD, D: Isabella Garlati
AD: Michele Salmi
P: Davide Cerati
Agency: Oikos Associati Visual Communication
SB: Oikos Associati sas

b 雑誌 Magazine UK 2006

CL: DIAD
AD: Vince Frost
D: Anthony Donovan / Ben Backhouse
CW: Lakshmi
DF, SB: Frost Design

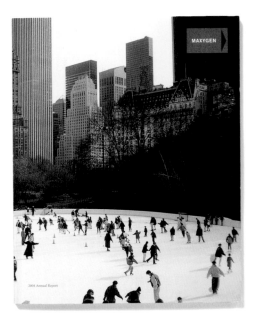

アニュアルレポート　Annual Report　USA　2005

CL: Maxygen
AD: Bill Cahan
D: Benjamine Morrison
DF, SB: Cahan & Associates

a

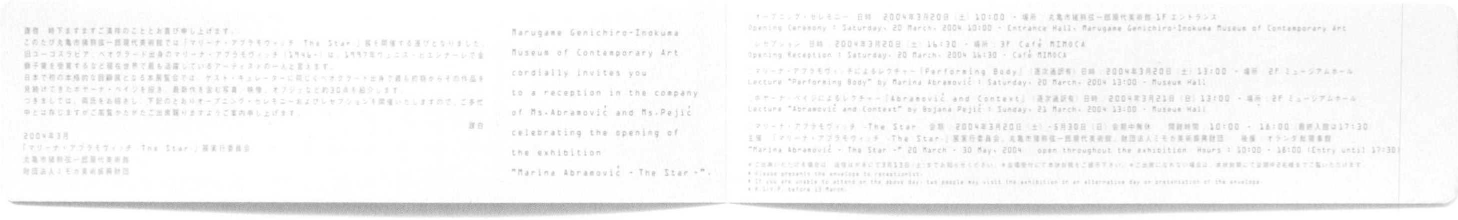

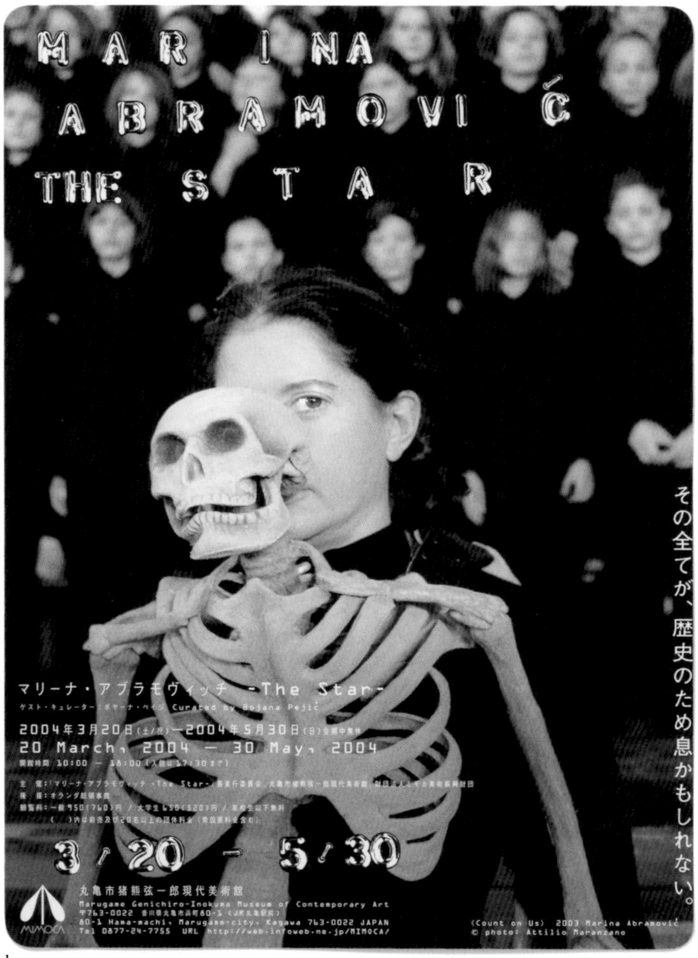

b

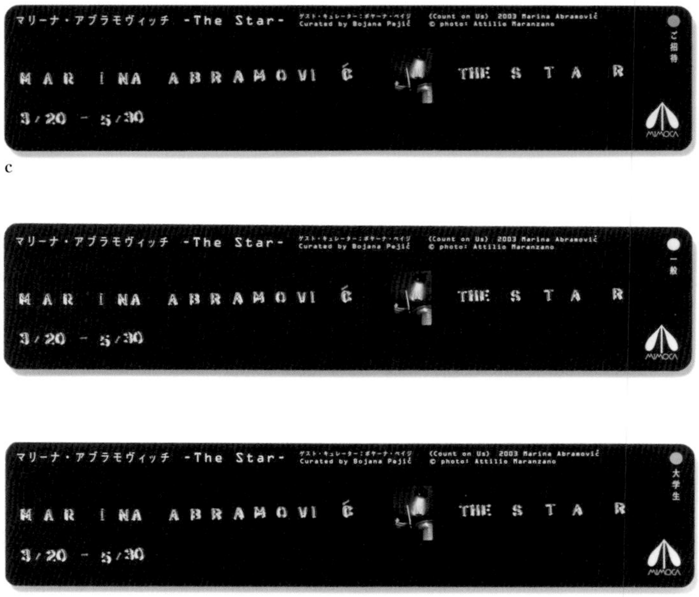

c

a 招待状. Invitation
b リーフレット Leaflet
c チケット Ticket　Japan　2004

CL: 丸亀市猪熊弦一郎現代美術館
　　Marugame Genichiro-Inokuma Museum of Contemporary Art
AD, D: 永井 裕明　Hiroaki Nagai
D: 栗原 幸治　Koji Kurihara
DF, SB: エヌ・ジー　N.G. Inc.

新聞 Newspaper Germany 2005

TIME TO RUN.

TIME TO RUN.

新聞 **Newspaper** Germany 2005
CL: Lauflunge
Chief Creative Director: Burkhart Von Scheven
CD: Stephan Ganser
AD: Daniel Hesse
P: Thomas Strogalski
CW: Bastian Engbert
Agency, SB: Jung Von Matt Ag

a

b

a ポスター Poster Germany 2004
CL: Campina
CD: Vappu Singer, Anke Winschewski
Art: Christine Manger, Rita Scholz
Account-Mgt: Jan Kowalsky
DF, SB: KNSK Werbeagentur GmbH, GWA

b ポスター Poster Germany 2004
CL: Media Academy Stuttgart
AD: Volker Schrader / Antje Hubsch
P: Bernd Mayer
CW: Harald Linsenmeier / Jorg Hoffmann
Agency, SB: McCann Erickson BCA GmbH

a

b

a メニューカバー **Menu Cover** Japan 2007
CL: ベージュ アラン・デュカス東京 BEIGE ALAIN DUCASSE TOKYO
AD: 美澤 修 Osamu Misawa
D: 竹田 麻衣子 Maiko Takeda
SB: 美澤修デザイン室 osamu misawa designroom Co., Ltd.

b 雑誌 **Magazine** Japan 2005
CL: D-NET
AD, D: 山田 英二 Eiji Yamada
DF, SB: ウルトラグラフィックス ULTRA Graphics

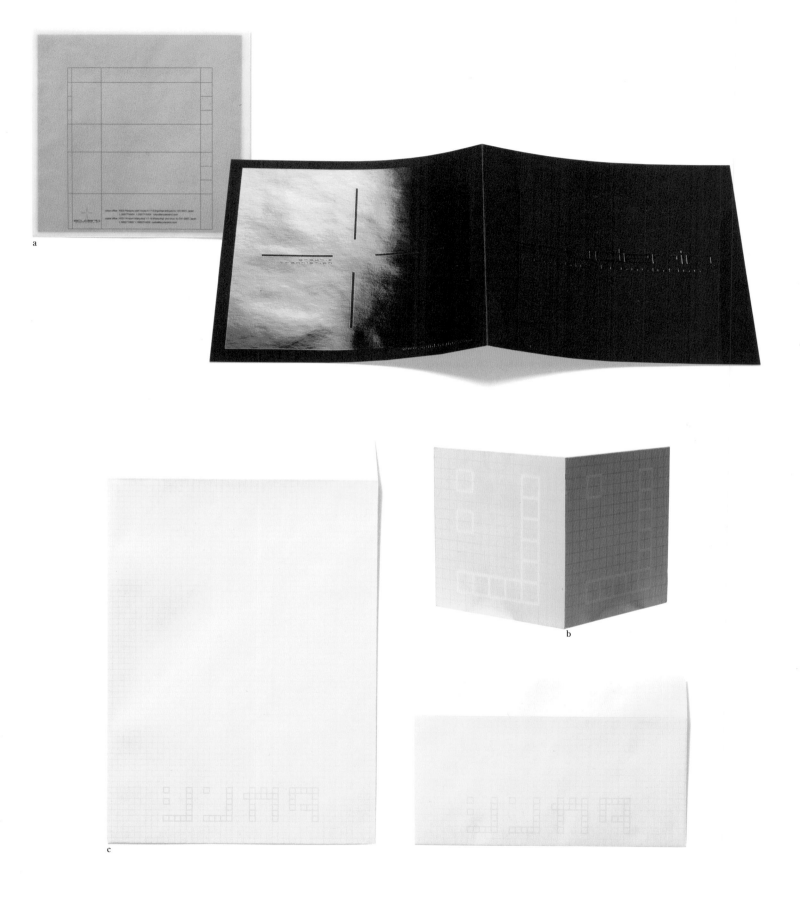

b 会社案内 Company Brochure
c 封筒 Envelope Japan 2004

CL, SB: シンガタ Shingata Inc.
AD: 水口 克夫 Katsuo Mizuguchi / 水野 学 Manabu Mizuno
　　副田 高行 Takayuki Soeda
D: 板倉 敬子 Keiko Itakura / 貝塚 智子 Tomoko Kaizuka
CW: 佐々木 宏 Hiroshi Sasaki / 萩原 ゆか Yuka Hagiwara

a ポートフォリオカバー Portfolio Cover Japan 2003

CL, SB: スクーデリア scuderia inc.
AD, D: 前田 義生 Yoshio Maeda

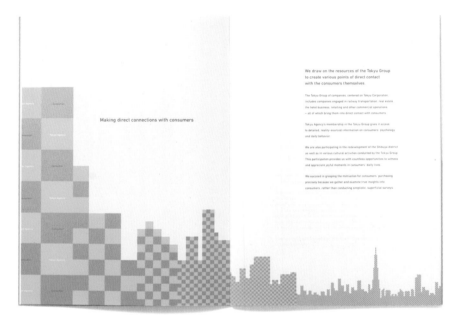

会社案内　Company Brochure　Japan　2006
CL, Agency, SB: 東急エージェンシー　Tokyu Agency Inc.
CD, CW: 藤本 修二　Syuji Fujimoto
AD: 福島 寛　Hiroshi Fukushima / 池澤 樹　Tastuki Ikezawa
D: 岩島 昭子　Akiko Iwashima
DF: タイドインク　TIDE Inc.

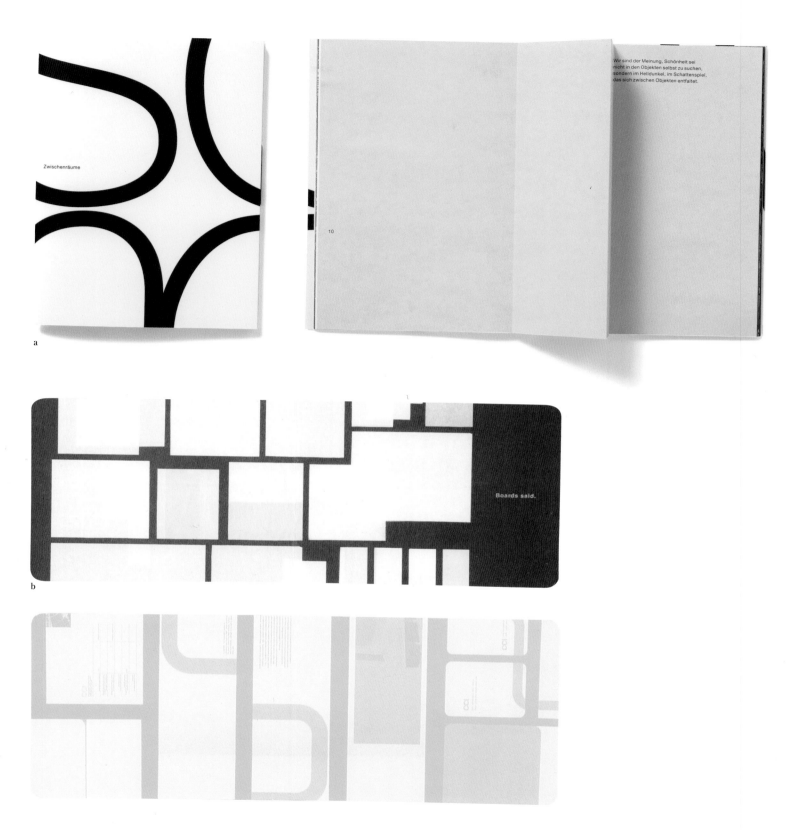

a ニューイヤーブックレット
New Year Booklet Austria 2006

CL, DF, SB: Felder Grafikdesign
AD, D: Peter Felder / Maria Mascher
P: Georg Alfare / Rene Dalpra / Albrecht Schnabel / Matthias Schrader
    Melissa Farlow / Hanspeter Schiess
CW: Gerhard Pirner / Jost Hochuli

b 書籍 Book Japan 2003

CL, SB: 松下計デザイン室　KEI Matsushita Design Room Inc.
CD, AD, D: 松下 計　Kei Matsusita

COESIA is a family held company controlling a multinational portfolio of automated machinery business featuring a leading position in different industries:
- food and beverage packaging
- tobacco making and packing
- chemical packaging
- hygiene disposables making and packaging
- five-axis milling machinery for aerospace and automotive applications
In addition to its automated machinery business, COESIA also detains a leading position in:
- gears and transmissions for high performance applications in the automotive industry

The development of solutions for handling materials with great accuracy and at high speed is the core competence of the COESIA Group companies. The Group's distinctive feature lies in its high investments in innovation: each year, 10% of the Group's turnover is dedicated to R & D.

Who we are: the power of knowledge

Over 7,000 customers served and 40,000 machines delivered worldwide are the evidence of the commitment to providing value-creating solutions in all sectors in which COESIA Group companies operate.

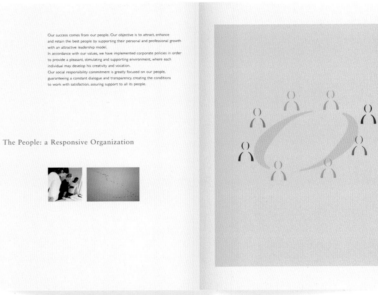

Our success comes from our people. Our objective is to attract, enhance and retain the best people by supporting their personal and professional growth with an attractive leadership model.
In accordance with our values, we have implemented corporate policies in order to provide a pleasant, stimulating and supporting environment, where each individual may develop his creativity and vocation.
Our social responsibility commitment is greatly focused on our people, guaranteeing a constant dialogue and transparency, creating the conditions to work with satisfaction, assuring support to all its people.

The People: a Responsive Organization

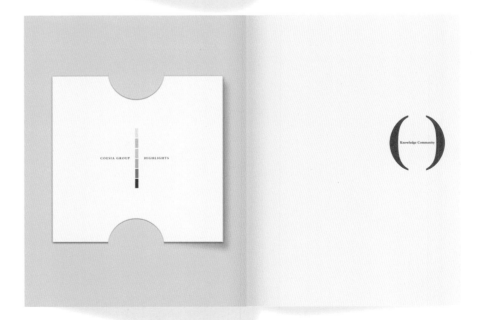

会社案内 **Company Brochure** Italy 2005
CL: Coesia Group
AD: Massimilano Sagrati
D: Hanna Lentinen
DF, SB: Carre Noir - Roma

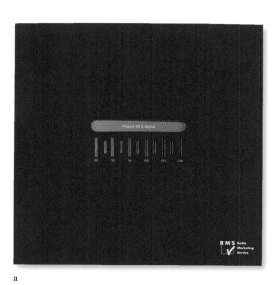

a

a フォルダー Folder　Germany　2003
CL: RMS Radio Marketing Service Gmb H 8 Co.KG
AD: Michael Deckelmann
Agency, DF: Campaneros Werbeagentur
SB: Campaneros Werbeagentur Gmb H

b ブローシャー Brochure
c チケット Ticket　USA　2003
CL: New Mexico Advertising Federation
AD: Robert E. Goldie
D: Lorenzo Romero / Zeke Sikelianos
Agency, DF, SB: Romeo & Gold Creative

b

c

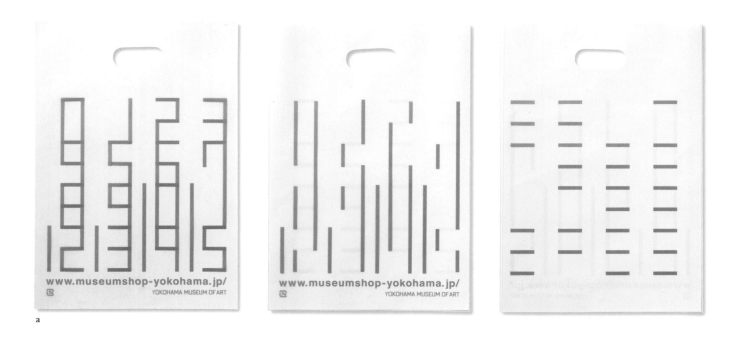

a

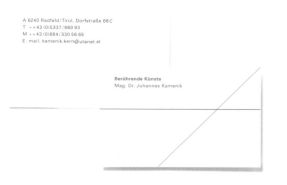

b

a ショップバッグ Shop Bag Japan 2004
CL: 横浜美術館ミュージアムショップ
　　Museum Shop of Yokohama Museum of Art
CD, AD, D: 高橋 正実 Masami Takahashi
DF, SB: マサミデザイン MASAMI DESIGN

b ステーショナリー Stationery Austria 2002
CL: Mag. Dr. Johannes Kamenik (Tai Chi Master)
AD, D: Peter Felder
DF, SB: Felder Grafikdesign
Print: Offset, 3c and Watermark

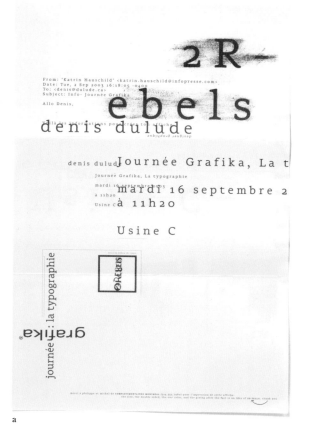

a

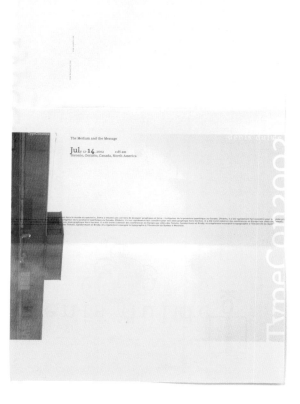

b

a, bポスター Poster Canada 2003 (a), 2002 (b)
CL, AD, D, P: Denis Dulude
DF, SB: Dulude Design

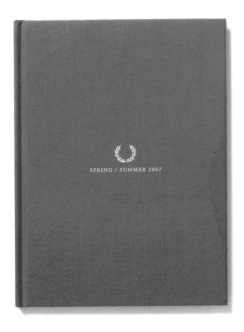

カタログ Catalogue　Japan　2007
CL: フレッドペリー　FRED PERRY
CD: 祐真 朋樹　Tomoki Sukezane
D: 吉村 亮　Ryo Yoshimura
P: 角田 みどり　Midori Tsunoda (model photography)
　　竹内 泰久　Yasuhisa Takenouchi
DF: 龍明堂　Ryu Ho Do
SB: ヒットユニオン　Hit Union

リーフレット **Leaflet** Japan 2007
CL: ユニバーサル ランゲージ UNIVERSAL LANGUAGE
CD, AD: 鈴木 克彦 Katsuhiko Suzuki
D: 館林 宏樹 Hiroki Tatebayashi / 堀川 剛 Takeshi Horikawa
P: 西田 宗之 Muneyuki Nishida
CW: 嵐田 光 Hikaru Arashida / 伊藤 毅 Takeshi Ito
Agency, SB: 博報堂 HAKUHODO Inc.

パッケージ **Package** Japan 2004

CL: 貝印 Kai corporation
CD, AD, D: コンドヲ トヨカズ Toyokazu Kondo
D: 片山 真輔 Shinsuke Katayama / 内田 慎吾 Shingo Uchida
P: 日置 武晴 Takeharu Hioki
CW: 坂東 真弓 Mayumi Bando
Stylist: 高橋 みどり Midori Takahashi
Producer: 長村 陽介 Yosuke Osamura
SB: アドビジョン Advision Co., Ltd.

a

b

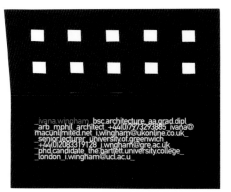

c

a パッケージ Package　Japan 2007

CL: ゴンチャロフ製菓　Goncharoff Confectionery Co., Ltd.
CD: ゴンチャロフ製菓 企画部　Goncharoff Planning Dept.
AD, D: 永島 学　Manabu Nagashima
D: 高山 マキコ　Makiko Takayama
SB: 永島学デザイン室　Manabu Nagashima Design Inc.

b 名刺 Business Card　England 2005

CL: Archtect Ivana Wingham
AD, D, CW: Edvard Čehovin
DF, SB: Design Center Ltd.

c ペーパーバッグ Paper Bag　Japan 2007

CL, DF, SB: アーサー・ハンドレッド・カンパニー　ASA 100 COMPANY
CD, AD: 浅埜 勝　Katsu Asano
AD: 米澤 帛笑　Kinue Yonezawa
D: 佐藤 瑞佳　Mizuka Sato / 笠原 碧　Midori Kasahara
Agency: ハンド イン ハンド　HAND in HAND

SUBMITTORS

GRAPHIC SIMPLICITY

シンプルグラフィックス

Jacket Design

スクーデリア　scuderia inc.

Designer

高松 セリア サユリ　Célia Sayuri Takamatsu

Editor

朴 清子　Sayoko Boku
及川 さえ子　Saeco Oikawa

Photographer

藤本 邦治　Kuniharu Fujimoto

Special Thanks

小間 浩子　Hiroko Koma
白倉 三紀子　Mikiko Shirakura
おりはら やすこ　Yasuko Orihara

Publisher

三芳 伸吾　Shingo Miyoshi

2007年8月6日　初版第1刷発行

発行所　ピエ・ブックス
〒170-0005　東京都豊島区南大塚2-32-4
編集 Tel: 03-5395-4820　Fax: 03-5395-4821
e-mail: editor@piebooks.com
営業 Tel: 03-5395-4811　Fax: 03-5395-4812
e-mail: sales@piebooks.com
http://www.piebooks.com

印刷・製本　株式会社サンニチ印刷